⎙ **W9-BXO-051**

Smart AND Spineless

EXPLORING INVERTEBRATE INTELLIGENCE

ANN DOWNER

TWENTY-FIRST CENTURY BOOKS / MINNEAPOLIS

Text copyright © 2016 by Ann Downer

All rights reserved. International copyright secured. No part of this book may
be reproduced, stored in a retrieval system, or transmitted in any form or by any
means—electronic, mechanical, photocopying, recording, or otherwise—without
the prior written permission of Lerner Publishing Group, Inc., except for the
inclusion of brief quotations in an acknowledged review.

Twenty-First Century Books
A division of Lerner Publishing Group, Inc.
241 First Avenue North
Minneapolis, MN 55401 USA

For reading levels and more information, look up this title at www.lernerbooks.com.

Main body text set in Aldus LT Std 11/15. Typeface provided by Adobe Systems.

Library of Congress Cataloging-in-Publication Data

Downer, Ann, 1960–
     Smart and spineless : exploring invertebrate intelligence / by Ann Downer.
         pages cm
     Includes bibliographical references and index.
     ISBN 978-1-4677-3739-5 (lib. bdg. : alk. paper)
     ISBN 978-1-4677-8805-2 (EB pdf)
     1. Invertebrates—Psychology—Juvenile literature. I. Title.
     QL362.4.D69 2016
     592.13—dc23   2014025658

Manufactured in the United States of America
1 – VP – 7/15/15

Contents

INTRODUCTION

Honey bees are key pollinators in the flowering plant world. Through physical contact, bees transfer pollen grains (the male sex cells of a flower) to the stigma (the female organ of a flower), a critical role in plant reproduction. Bees are amazingly intelligent. They can learn new concepts and are able to understand abstract thought.

When you think of smart animals, what comes to mind? Wise old owls? Problem-solving dolphins? Maybe you think of famous animals like Koko the gorilla, who has mastered one thousand signs in American Sign Language, or YouTube celebrity Chaser the border collie, who recognizes one thousand different English names for her stuffed toys.

But what about the ants on the sidewalk or the bees pollinating flowers in the park? What about the octopus and the jellyfish on the other side of the glass at the aquarium? Are insects, spiders, and other animals without backbones smart too?

When we think of intelligent creatures, we often think of vertebrates, or animals with spinal columns and relatively large brains. We don't generally think of invertebrates, or animals without a spine. But invertebrates can be astonishingly intelligent. These animals exhibit feats of learning, memory, and problem solving using their relatively simple, tiny brains—some no bigger than a sesame seed, some even smaller. In fact, some invertebrates have no brain at all!

Scientists around the world are putting invertebrate intelligence to use in mind-boggling ways worthy of a science fiction movie. Engineers are designing swarmbots (robot swarms) based on bees to take part in search and rescue efforts. And materials scientists are basing a new, tough ceramic on the structure of a mantis shrimp's claw.

JUST WHAT IS AN INVERTEBRATE, ANYWAY?

If it's an animal on Earth that you can see without a microscope, chances are good you're looking at an invertebrate. That's because more than 90 percent of animal life on our planet consists of invertebrates. These spineless creatures—such as spiders and earthworms—far outnumber the animals with backbones, which include fishes, amphibians, reptiles, birds, and mammals. Yet it's easy to overlook invertebrates. We notice vertebrates without any trouble, whether it's the neighbor walking a dog, a pigeon roosting on a utility line, or a squirrel scampering up a tree. But we tend to pay less attention to smaller, less familiar life-forms. Invertebrates tend to be smaller than your little finger—often much smaller—and they can live in dark, out-of-the-way places. We may have to dig through the compost bin or flip over a brick or turn on the porch light to find them.

Insects, spiders, shrimps, crabs, and lobsters are all examples of invertebrates. They are arthropods, a big group of segmented animals with jointed legs and an exoskeleton, or outer skeleton. But non-arthropods such

WHAT IS A BRAIN?

A brain is an organ that makes it possible for vertebrates and invertebrates to move, sense, and otherwise function during life. For a long time, scientists viewed cognition (thinking) as the sole province of vertebrates, but recent studies have shown that some invertebrates can apply knowledge from experience to new problems, a key component of thought. The human brain has 86 billion neurons—or nerve cells, the main type of cell in the brain. By contrast, the honey bee brain has only 960,000 neurons. Yet even with fewer neurons, the honey bee is capable of abstract thought, is able to learn concepts, and can remember which abstract symbol will result in reward or punishment.

In honey bee experiments conducted between 2008 and 2010, for example, Aurore Avarguès-Weber at the University of Toulouse in France showed that bees could learn to associate an abstract symbol with a sweet-tasting reward or a bitter-tasting punishment. Even though the symbols were changed throughout the experiment, the bees were able to learn the concepts of "above-below" and "different" and could remember which abstract symbol resulted in sweet sugar water.

Should we continue to try to understand invertebrate brains by looking to the vertebrate standard? Maybe not. For one thing, while invertebrate brains may be small, they have a higher number of different types of neurons than do vertebrates. This diversity allows them to fine-tune their behavior to various conditions. Yet big brains do have benefits. Humans can scan a complex scene in under ten milliseconds—ten thousandths of a second. This is the result of powerful parallel processing in the brain. As a person's senses make order of the flood of sensation, more than one part of the brain is at work to make sense of things.

As far as scientists know, bees and other invertebrates can't parallel process. Their brains are too small. In evolutionary terms, they made a trade-off, giving up the ability to parallel process in exchange for a miniature brain. As a result, invertebrates have to figure out their world in real time.

invertebrates

ANIMALS ANIMALS ANIMALS

vertebrates

plants

fungi

protists

monerans

Most animals on Earth (more than 90 percent) are invertebrates. This illustrated pie chart shows the extent to which invertebrate life dominates other life-forms, including plants and humans and other vertebrates.

as worms and snails and slugs are invertebrates too. Cnidarians such as jellyfish and corals are too. So are mollusks such as cuttlefish, octopus, and squid. What makes something an invertebrate is what it *doesn't* have: an internal vertebral column, often just simply called a spine, or a backbone.

WHAT DOES IT MEAN TO BE SMART?

Intelligence is sometimes confused with instinct. Both vertebrates and invertebrates exhibit instinctual behaviors, or actions that an organism carries out without conscious thought. But can invertebrates, with their simple and mostly tiny brains, show signs of intelligence? In recent years, scientists have conducted experiments in the field as well as in the lab, showing how some invertebrates solve puzzles and problems, plan detours, evade obstacles, recognize nestmates, choose new homes, and play. Some invertebrates even have personalities. However, intelligence in a spineless creature doesn't look like intelligence in a chimpanzee or a dolphin, or even in the family dog. But invertebrates do exhibit some form of cognition, or conscious thought, which is defined as the use and handling of knowledge. Invertebrates use and handle knowledge all the time, in ways that go beyond instinct.

BIOLOGICAL CLASSIFICATION

Scientists classify life-forms into a hierarchical system that groups microbes, plants, and animals by shared traits. At the top of the classification hierarchy is the domain, to which a broad and wide range of animals belong based on a small number of similarities. From there, animals are grouped into narrower categories based on increasing amounts of similarity. From broadest to narrowest category, these groupings are kingdom, phylum, class, order, family, genus, and species. (You can remember the categories with this simple, funny mnemonic aid: **K**ing **P**hilip **C**ame **O**ver **F**or **G**ood **S**paghetti.)

NEIGHBOR'S DOG: CLASSIFICATION

KINGDOM: Animal

PHYLUM: Vertebrata (things with backbones)

CLASS: Mammalia (fur-covered animals that nourish their young with milk)

ORDER: Carnivora (meat eaters)

FAMILY: Canidae (wolves, foxes, and other dog-like meat eaters)

GENUS: *Canis* (dogs)

SPECIES: *familiaris* (domestic dogs)

INVERTEBRATE CLASSIFICATION

Biologists classify invertebrates into thirty phyla. Biologists have yet to describe many invertebrate species. The most common invertebrate phyla are these:

 ANNELIDA (26,000 SPECIES): These are segmented worms, many of which are found in the ocean. The most familiar are earthworms.

 ARTHROPODA (1,170,000 SPECIES): These are jointed animals—insects, spiders and other arachnids, myriapoda (centipedes and millipedes), and crustaceans—with an exoskeleton

 CNIDARIA (9,000 SPECIES): The root of this name is the Greek word for "nettle," a plant with stinging hairs. This phylum includes corals, anemones, jellyfishes, and freshwater hydrozoans. They all have special stinging cells called nematocysts that help them catch prey.

 ECHINODERMATA (7,000 SPECIES): In Greek *Echinodermata* means "hedgehog skin." Some members of this phylum have spiny skins (starfish, sand dollars, and sea urchins), while others do not (sea cucumbers and sea fans). All members of this phylum have an endoskeleton, a skeleton under the spiny skin, but no spine.

 MOLLUSCA (100,000 SPECIES): Some mollusks—snails, clams, paper nautilus, and tusk shells—have shells. Some—including slugs, colorful nudibranchs, and the cephalopods (squid, octopus, and cuttlefish)—do not. Most mollusks have a muscular foot. Cephalopods have tentacles.

 PORIFERA (25,800 SPECIES): Organisms in this phylum include natural sponges that live in the sea. Sponges are characterized by pores and channels, which allow water to flow through the animal.

CHAPTER ONE

THE NOT-SO-LOWLY WORM

Even with tiny brains, earthworms exhibit intelligence.
They are capable of learning and of figuring out solutions
to problems in their world through trial and error.

MEET THE EARTHWORM

COMMON NAMES: *Lumbricus terrestris* is commonly known as a nightcrawler, rainworm, dew worm, angleworm, squirrel tail, or twachel. *Diplocardia mississippiensis* is known as a grunt worm or a pink.

NICKNAME: None

WHAT SCIENTISTS CALL IT: *Lumbricus terrestris (L. terrestris)* and *Diplocardia mississippiensis (D. mississippiensis)*

RELATIVES: *L. terrestris* shares its family with about seven hundred other species. *D. mississippiensis* belongs to a family of four hundred species.

HOW BIG IS IT? *L. terrestris* is up to 9 inches (23 centimeters) long, and *D. mississippiensis* is up to 11.8 inches (30 cm) long.

WHERE'S HOME? In North America, *D. mississippiensis* is a native species, while *L. terrestris* is native to Europe and was later introduced to North America.

FAVORITE FOODS: It will eat almost anything that used to be alive. In nature, worms eat dead leaves and other organic matter breaking down in the soil. Earthworms have been known to eat cardboard, sawdust, coffee grounds, and eggshells. Some people keep worms indoors in bins, feeding them kitchen scraps to process into garden compost.

KNOWN FOR: It is known as an expert soil engineer. Through its tunneling and castings (worm feces), the earthworm naturally mixes air into the soil and enriches it. Well-oxygenated soil is good for growing plants of all kinds.

BRAIN SIZE: The earthworm brain consists of a fused pair of ganglia (nerve cells) in the third segment from the mouth. The two pear-shaped ganglia above the pharynx are considered the earthworm's brain.

How smart can any earthworm possibly be? Its brain is tiny, for one thing. Yet no less a thinker than English naturalist Charles Darwin spent decades studying worms.

Darwin rocked the world in 1859 when he published *On the Origin of Species,* a book outlining natural selection. In this scientific theory, Darwin explained that living things evolve over time. Creatures with features or differences that give them survival advantages pass on those features to the next generation. Over generations, these differences—often small—add up to an entirely new kind of plant or animal. Darwin's theory of evolution was radical. It challenged accepted religious doctrine as put forth in the Bible's Book of Genesis and spurred heated debate around the world. *On the Origin of Species* made Darwin internationally famous. Yet for the most part, he chose to live a quiet life with his wife and children at Down House, his country home in the village of Downe, just outside London, England. He spent his time reading, writing scientific papers and books, exchanging letters with scientists around the world, and conducting experiments about anything that interested him. One of those things was the earthworm.

ON WORM INTELLIGENCE

When he was an old man, Darwin was in his study one day with his family, most likely his wife, Emma (who played the piano), and his grown son Francis (who played the bassoon). Darwin had asked them to play music for some earthworms. The worms came from the gardens around Down House, and they were living in large flowerpots in Charles Darwin's study. Darwin later wrote in his book about earthworms, "As I was led to keep in my study during many months worms in pots filled with earth, I became interested in them, and wished to learn how far they acted consciously, and how much mental power they displayed."

In his account of the experiment, Darwin wrote this:

> Worms do not possess any sense of hearing. They took not the least notice of the shrill notes from a metal whistle, which was repeatedly sounded near them; nor did they of the

PLAYING THE PICCOLO FOR WORMS

At Harvard University in Cambridge, Massachusetts, Ned Friedman, a professor of evolutionary biology, and his students re-created some of Darwin's worm experiments in a new 2011 course called "Getting to Know Charles Darwin." They gather in a music hall to see whether earthworms will react to shouting, piano playing, or the notes from a piccolo. Like Darwin, the students observed no reaction to sound among the worms and concluded that worms have no sense of hearing.

deepest and loudest tones of a bassoon. They were indifferent to shouts, if care was taken that the breath did not strike them. When placed on a table close to the keys of a piano, which was played as loudly as possible, they remained perfectly quiet.

In a separate outdoor experiment, Darwin noted that although the worms paid no attention to sound, their tiny, simple brains could sense light. An earthworm exposed to bright light, he wrote, "dashes into its burrow like a rabbit." Was this just a reflex? Darwin didn't think so, because the worms didn't always make a dash for the burrow. Sometimes when they were busy doing something else, the worms failed to respond to a sudden bright light. If the worms could be distracted and thereby ignored the light, Darwin reasoned that they must be capable of paying attention—a behavior associated with animals with backbones and with much larger brains.

PUNCH'S FANCY PORTRAITS.—No. 54

CHARLES ROBERT DARWIN, LL.D., F.R.S.

IN HIS *DESCENT OF MAN* HE BROUGHT HIS OWN SPECIES DOWN AS LOW AS POSSIBLE—*I.E.*, TO "A HAIRY QUADRUPED FURNISHED WITH A TAIL AND POINTED EARS, AND PROBABLY *ARBOREAL* IN ITS HABITS"—WHICH IS A REASON FOR THE VERY GENERAL INTEREST IN A "FAMILY TREE." HE HAS LATELY BEEN TURNING HIS ATTENTION TO THE "POLITIC WORM."

An 1881 cartoon in the British weekly magazine *Punch* lampoons Charles Darwin for his latest scientific obsession—earthworms. Darwin was keenly interested in discovering whether worms acted through reflex or through intelligence. His research was part of a larger body of work that eventually proved that worms do possess a form of intelligence.

And just what were the worms doing that distracted them from noticing the bright light? They were dragging leaves into their burrows in Darwin's garden. Darwin had some ideas about why they might be doing this. They might be dragging leaves into the burrows to use for food or for warm lining. Or they might be creating a plug to keep out water or birds and other predators. Through observation, Darwin concluded that the worms were using leaves as a type of natural plug. And he noticed that the worms seemed to prefer to draw the leaves into the burrow by their pointy tips. He conducted an experiment in which he offered the worms paper triangles instead of leaves. Even though there were many more places to grab the triangle along its broad base, the worms were twice as likely to pull the triangles into their burrows by one of the pointy corners.

Darwin also noticed that when the worms couldn't find leaves to plug the burrow entrance, they would fill it with small stones. When he pulled the stones out of the burrow openings, Darwin saw the worms reach out of the burrow to drag the stones back with their mouths!

INSTINCT OR INTELLIGENCE?

Were these worm behaviors instinct or intelligence? Or was it pure chance?

Darwin didn't think it was instinct, and he eventually abandoned the idea of random chance. How could instinct or chance help the worms figure out how to grab objects such as paper triangles, which they had never before encountered? In addition, many of the trees in English gardens such as Darwin's were not native to the region so their leaves would not be something the worms would recognize. Darwin concluded that because earthworms displayed the ability to react differently and

INSTINCT VS. INTELLIGENCE

Instinct is something that biologists describe as preprogrammed tendencies essential to a species' survival. A lot of instinctual behaviors, including the migration of monarch butterflies, are regulated by hormones. An automatic reflex is an instinctive, unlearned reaction to a stimulus. When a doctor whacks a person's knee with a rubber hammer, for example, and the leg jerks up, that is an automatic reflex.

Intelligence, on the other hand, refers to the ability to benefit and learn from experience and to apply that information to new situations. Key components of intelligence are memory and learning. Learning by trial and error is a form of learning wherein an animal tries many different reactions to a situation, seemingly at random, until one is successful. Darwin's earthworms used trial and error to pull leaves into their burrows.

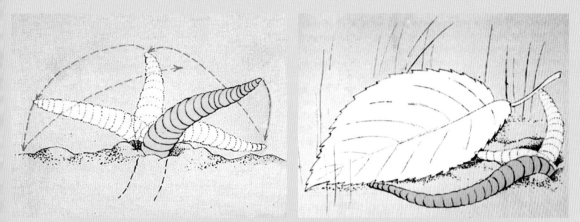

In the early 1900s, Hermann Jordan, a Dutch naturalist, observed that in plugging the entrance to its underground burrow, an earthworm comes only partway out of the entrance *(left)* to do the job. And to pull a leaf into the burrow, the worm often changes its grip on the leaf for the most efficient angle *(right)*. This ability to adjust for a better result is a sign of intelligence.

successfully to a range of unfamiliar elements, the animals must have some form of simple intelligence.

But that didn't turn out to be the final answer. Decades after Darwin's worm experiments, Dutch naturalist Hermann Jordan did something Darwin and others hadn't: he watched worm behavior at night, with the aid of a lantern. He saw that to create a plug, a worm didn't actually come all the way out of its burrow but instead emerged only partway. It would explore all around its burrow until it felt a leaf and would then try to pull it in, sometimes successfully and sometimes not. Jordan reported that the worms were very persistent. They would try over and over again until they succeeded in pulling a leaf into their burrow. Jordan observed that the worms were most successful when they happened to grab a leaf by its pointy tip. Through his observations, Jordan concluded that the worms were relying not on reflex but on a method of trial and error, an idea Darwin had considered but eventually abandoned.

So are worms intelligent or not? In about 1912, around the same time Jordan was observing worms with his lantern, American psychologist Robert Yerkes was putting earthworms into a simple T-shaped maze as part of his work on intelligence testing. One arm of the maze was lined with sandpaper and led to a device that delivered a mild electric shock. The other

Robert Yerkes (1876–1956) was a psychologist and primatologist known for his work studying intelligence in humans and primates. He also studied the intelligence of worms, determining that they have the capacity for simple learning. He is pictured here in 1929 at his desk at Yale University.

arm of the maze was smooth and led to the safety of a burrow. Over time, Yerkes's worms came to associate the rough sandpaper with the electric shock. They avoided the arm of the maze with the sandpaper and, instead, sought out the smooth arm leading to the burrow. From this experiment, Yerkes concluded that worms are capable of simple learning, which is a basic form of intelligence. Worms manage to learn with a brain that is just two tiny fused neurons.

GRUNTING FOR WORMS

In Sopchoppy, Florida, worm grunting—a method of attracting worms out of the ground to use for bait—confirms one of Darwin's nineteenth-century observations. In his earthworm experiments, Darwin had noticed that worms appear to be deaf to sounds carried through the air. However, they reacted to vibration, quickly retreating into their burrows when they felt vibrations. Twenty-first-century Florida worm grunting involves driving a wooden stake into the ground and rubbing it with a metal file to create vibrations. The local worms (*Diplocardia mississippiensis*) come pouring out of the ground by the bucketsful!

Ken Catania, a biology professor at Vanderbilt University in Nashville, Tennessee, theorizes that the worm-grunter vibrations resemble those set up by one of the worms' chief predators: the eastern American mole. As the mole digs into a worm burrow, looking for a worm dinner, the digging movement sends vibrations into the burrows, panicking the worms. Trying to flee the moles, the worms scurry out of their burrows, where predators easily catch them. Catania also notes that two other worm predators, wood turtles and herring gulls, have figured out how to imitate the vibrations of tunneling moles to lure worms.

Amy Stokley, a Florida worm-grunting queen, rubs a metal file over a wooden stake in the ground to create the vibrations that will lure earthworms out of the ground.

CHAPTER TWO

JUMPING SPIDERS: PORTIA

Portia fimbriata, a type of jumping spider, is known for its natural ability to camouflage itself, blending seamlessly into its surroundings. The spider is also known for its intelligence, based in part on its vision. In this image, six of its eyes are visible.

MEET PORTIA THE JUMPING SPIDER

COMMON NAME: It is called a fringed jumping spider.

NICKNAMES: Its nicknames are eight-legged cat and Portia.

WHAT SCIENTISTS CALL IT: *Portia fimbriata* (*P. fimbriata*)

RELATIVES: The genus to which *P. fimbriata* belongs includes as many as sixteen other species, which live in Australia, Southeast Asia, and Africa.

HOW BIG IS PORTIA? Females are about ⅓ inch (8.4 millimeters) long. Males are only about ¼ inch (6.4 mm) long.

WHERE'S HOME? It lives in the rain forests of Queensland, Australia, as well as Southeast Asia.

FAVORITE FOODS: It eats other spiders and the eggs of other fringed jumping spiders.

KNOWN FOR: It is known for crazy camouflage, fabulous eyesight, and sneaky hunting techniques.

BRAIN SIZE: Its brain is not much bigger than a poppy seed and is packed with six hundred thousand neurons.

Meet Portia. Or, to call her by her full scientific name, *Portia fimbriata* (*P. fimbriata*). (To scientists, *Portia*—in italics—always refers to all the species in the scientific genus *Portia*. In this chapter, "Portia" is shorthand just for *P. fimbriata*, the fringed jumping spider.) *Fimbriata* means "fringed" and refers to the brown, gray, and white hairs that camouflage this spider's body and legs. Spiders in the genus *Portia* live in Australia and Southeast Asia. They eat other spiders, most of them much bigger than they are. They manage this in astonishing ways, both by actively hunting for their prey and by building webs that trap other food sources.

Portia is a jumping spider, and like all other spiders, she has eight legs. She uses these legs to pounce on her prey, and she is such a good hunter that some researchers call her an "eight-legged cat." Also to her advantage as a predator is her heavy body camouflage. Portia is mottled in shades of hard-to-see brown and gray and white, and her fringes create an uneven, confusing body silhouette that is hard for other spiders to see. Most web-building spiders have poor eyesight, so they rely on vibrations through the

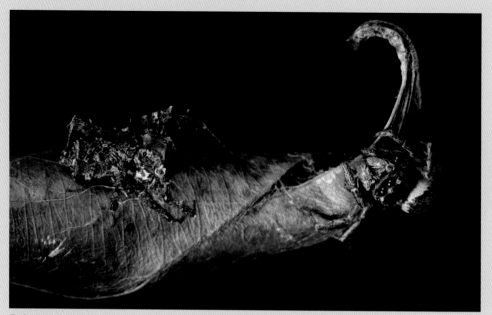

P. fimbriata *(left)* lures another type of jumping spider—a female *Euryattus Thorell sp. indet.* *(right)*—from her suspension nest in a curled-up leaf. Portia does this by using her smarts to mimic the vibratory, leaf-rocking courtship behavior of the male *Euryattus*.

silk strands of their webs to tell them that prey—or an intruder—is on the web. Portia, on the other hand, has excellent eyesight. She can easily and quickly spot her prey well before they are aware of her presence.

Portia is also what scientists call an aggressive mimic. When she attacks the web of a prey spider, she adopts behaviors that deceive or lure the prey toward her. For example, when she is invading a web, she uses the wind as a smokescreen to mask her own movements, advancing with a breeze and stopping when the breeze dies down. Once on the spider prey's web, she can walk in a jerky, robotic fashion to resemble windblown trash that the prey would want to investigate, coming within easy reach of Portia's fangs. She also uses her legs to shake the web to imitate a struggling fly or a male spider in courting mode. When the prey spider comes to investigate, Portia strikes.

PORTIA TAKES A DETOUR

Scientists have been studying Portia and her tricks for decades. One astonishing observation happened back in 1987. Two animal behaviorists,

Stimson (Stim) Wilcox from Binghamton University in New York and Robert Ray Jackson from the University of Canterbury in New Zealand, had traveled to Australia in December (Australia's summer) to learn what sneaky signals Portia was using to trick her prey. To carry out their research, Wilcox and Jackson headed into the rain forest of the state of Queensland in northeastern Australia, where the fringed jumping spider lives. Wilcox had equipment to measure vibrations on spiderwebs, and the scientists also had a hungry *Portia fimbriata* in a plastic vial. The plan was to place Portia in the web of a prey spider and then observe Portia's predatory behaviors. Jackson remembers, "We found a web conveniently situated on the trunk of a large rain forest tree. Stim got his [recording] gadgets out and set everything up so that we could record [vibrations] off the web."

The web belonged to a spider called *Argiope appensa*. *Argiope* is an orb weaver, a spider that builds round webs with spokes of sticky spider silk that meet at the center. Orb weaver spiders sit in the middle of their webs, waiting for insects to fly into them and get caught in the sticky silk. Spider webs are made of both sticky and nonsticky silk, however, and Portia is careful not to walk on the sticky silk, so she does not get stuck in the web.

Jackson wrote, "We planned to let Portia walk out of the vial and on to the tree trunk a short distance below the web. We thought Portia would see the orb weaver, and then walk up the tree trunk and into the web. Then, with Portia in the web, we could record her signals. Simple."

Or so he and Wilcox thought. Jackson explained that "we opened the vial and Portia walked out slowly, stopped and looked up at the web, but she didn't walk up the tree trunk to the web. Instead, Portia looked all around. And then she walked away. We assumed our morning had been a failure."

NEXT STEPS

The two scientists discussed what to do next. In the hot, humid rain forest, Jackson and Wilcox were slow to pack up and move out. After twenty minutes had passed, Jackson happened to look up, and to his surprise, he saw Portia on a vine hanging over the *Argiope appensa*'s web. The scientists watched to see what would happen next.

Jackson recalls that "Portia fastened a line of silk to the vine and then dropped down slowly, holding onto the dragline [a length of silk that functions as a rappelling rope, for the spider's safety], descending parallel to the orb web, but not touching it. When she was aligned with the *Argiope appensa* at the hub, Portia began to swing on the silk line—at first only lightly, but eventually working up momentum. Then, wham! Portia swung onto the resting *Argiope*."

That was the end for the hapless orb weaver. The two scientists watched as Portia sat at the web's center, eating the prey spider. Jackson and Wilcox were astounded. Portia had given no signal that she was planning a detour. And she had not even touched the web until the very last moment, when she was ready to attack the spider. How had Portia known to adapt her behavior and switch to another stealthier approach?

Jackson and Wilcox wanted to learn more about what they had just witnessed. They discovered that the *Argiope appensa* orb weaver is an expert at interpreting web vibrations and other signals. It is adept at telling whether web signals are from prey or from dangerous web invaders. Jackson explains that "when *Argiope appensa* gets signals that might be from a

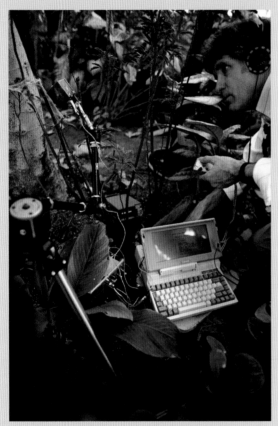

Animal behaviorist Stimson Wilcox measures spider web vibrations in the rain forest of northeastern Australia as part of a study of spider intelligence. Through his work with *P. fimbriata*, he has observed the spider's ability to adapt behavior to circumstances, another key sign of intelligence.

potential predator, it rapidly flexes its legs, making the web shake violently. Would-be predators like Portia, when they walk into the web, lose their footing [because they don't walk on the sticky silk], and are even thrown off on to the forest floor."

WAS PORTIA MAKING A PLAN?

At that time, less was known about invertebrate intelligence, and Portia's defeat of the *Argiope* defenses was unnerving to Jackson and Wilcox. They wondered how she had so effectively adopted a seemingly new strategy to attack her prey. The scientists had observed the way Portia had initially looked at the spider in the web and then walked off in a different direction. But then later, Portia had maneuvered to be in exactly the right position, attached to the vine above the web, to attack her prey. Jackson recalls, "Seeing this [behavior] planted a scary question in my head. Did Portia see the vine over the web and make a plan? When Portia walked away, was she beginning a planned detour to a specific goal? That sounds like proposing that a spider was *thinking*. Back then, that was a scary idea."

In 1987 some scientists weren't even willing to credit vertebrate animals with the power of thought. As for a spider? That seemed crazy. "We wondered whether we should just keep such ideas to ourselves," Jackson remembers.

PORTIA THINKS WITH HER EYES

Instead, Jackson and Wilcox continued their studies of Portia's behavior. Duane Harland, one of Jackson's former graduate students, was busy trying to "get under the hood of these tiny geniuses," to learn just how Portia sized up potential prey. In the early 2000s, Harland conducted experiments in the spider lab at the University of Canterbury to tease out the tiny cues Portia was reading to determine what kind of spider or insect she was facing in her hunt. For Portia, getting it wrong could mean ending up as another spider's dinner.

Through his experiments, Harland realized that the size of Portia's brain wasn't what made her such an adaptive hunter. In fact, Portia's brain is not much bigger than a poppy seed. He discovered that Portia was thinking

P. fimbriata thinks with its eyes. In other words, its brain has a large region devoted to processing visual information. Jumping spiders have excellent vision, among the best in invertebrates. Four of the spider's eight eyes are on its face (two in the center and two to the side). The other four are on the spider's carapace, or outer shell. The two big eyes in the center see extremely clearly, but only across a small area. The other six eyes see less well but across a much broader area.

with her eyes. "Complex decisions are not always made by brains," Harland says. "Some animals make decisions with their eyes. How smart are Portia's eyes? Like Portia's behavior, Portia's eyes are surprisingly complex and include intricate eye movements." The eyes on the side of Portia's head track movement, while her large, front-facing eyes detect depth. Her motion-detecting eyes help her spot her prey in its web, and great depth perception helps her judge how far to leap. With eyes at the sides of her head, Portia pretty much has 360-degree vision.

Elizabeth Jakob at the University of Massachusetts Amherst is also working on tracking jumping-spider vision with a different species. With a team of colleagues from around the world, Jakob is building a spider eye tracker, a high-tech piece of lab equipment to reveal just how jumping spiders think with their eyes and make decisions. "It's like having a window into a spider's brain," she says.

Later experiments by Michael Tarsitano showed that this tiny spider can indeed make and act on plans. He showed that Portia uses different strategies depending on the sizes of the spider she perceives in the web. He positioned two dead gray house spiders of different sizes in lifelike postures in an orb web. Then he watched what Portia did. She followed these rules:

1. If the resident spider is small, imitate an insect struggling in the web.
2. If the resident spider is large, imitate an insect brushing against the edge of the web. This will keep the resident spider out of the web and spare Portia from becoming the large spider's dinner.
3. If entering in the resident spider's web, regardless of the resident spider's size, mask footsteps with a vibratory smokescreen. For example, move forward when the breeze is blowing.

In the end, it's hard to escape the conclusion that Portia is a very intelligent spider.

CHAPTER THREE

OCTOPUSES

Octopuses, such as this *Octopus vulgaris*, display a wide range of behaviors that exhibit intelligence. They solve puzzles, figure out how to escape enclosed spaces, make tools, have personalities—and more amazingly, they play.

MEET THE COMMON OCTOPUS

COMMON NAME: It is called the common octopus.

NICKNAME: None

WHAT SCIENTISTS CALL IT: *Octopus vulgaris* (*O. vulgaris*)

RELATIVES: At least two hundred species of octopuses live in the world's oceans. They all live in salt water, though some larger octopuses are known to wander among tide pools. These smaller pools of water along the seashore appear at low tide, are less salty than ocean water, and provide habitat to all kinds of marine animals.

HOW BIG IS IT? It is 1 to 3 feet (.3 to .9 meters) long, including the arms.

WHERE'S HOME? Octopuses live in oceans worldwide. They spend the winters in deep water, migrating to shallow coastal water in the warmer months.

FAVORITE FOODS: Clams and crabs are favorite octopus foods. Octopuses create middens, or trash piles, outside their dens. By studying the middens, scientists can see what they have been eating.

KNOWN FOR: It is known for problem solving, escape artistry, and playful behavior.

BRAIN SIZE: The octopus brain has about 167 million neurons and another 333 million neurons divided among its arms. That's a total of 500 million neurons in the octopus nervous system—a respectable number for an animal with no spine. By contrast, a honey bee has only 960,000 neurons in its brain.

When you think of a brainy creature that lives in the sea, what comes to mind? A dolphin? A killer whale? These toothed marine mammals are certainly smart, but what if one of the brightest minds in the ocean actually was the octopus? Over the past few decades, scientists have been documenting just how smart octopuses are. These animals are masters of escape, which means they are a challenge to keep in captivity. They solve other types of puzzles in the natural world with ease. They make tools and they play. Octopuses may even have personalities.

ESCAPE ARTISTS

One researcher has called octopuses hyperactive Houdinis, after the legendary escape artist Harry Houdini. And they start their escapes when they are young. Octopus keepers around the world have found tiny octopus hatchlings escaping through the narrow plastic tubing of their tanks. Ian Gleadall, a marine biologist working at Tohoku University in Japan, recalls watching one large octopus that weighed about 6.5 pounds (3 kilograms) squeeze between two slats of a marine lab duckboard (a type of removable wooden flooring to hold items off wet floors). It then crawled away through the tiny gap between the duckboard and the underlying floor. "Even seeing it happen, it was difficult to believe an octopus could become so flat and still actively crawl!" Gleadall recalls.

PUZZLE SOLVERS

In 2012 fish ecologist Lauren de Vos of the Marine Research Institute at the University of Cape Town was studying the ocean life of False Bay on the southwestern coast of South Africa. De Vos was using a baited remote underwater video (BRUV) setup. This equipment consists of a canister baited with crushed sardines, secured to an underwater post with three cable ties. An underwater camera mounted nearby records the various marine animals that come to check out the bait. Researchers rely on BRUVs to track the number of creatures and different species in a particular area and to record their behaviors.

But octopuses have learned that BRUVs are fast food. When De Vos reviewed test footage one day, she saw an octopus swim up to the bait canister, fend off a striped cat shark with several of its arms, and use its free arms to undo the cable ties. Then it swam off with the bait canister!

Octopuses are amazing puzzle solvers, which scientists view as a sign of developed intelligence. And because octopuses are so smart, aquarists (the staff at aquariums who care for the animals) look for ways to provide stimulation for this smart animal. They might challenge the octopus to retrieve a live crab in a jar, sealed inside another jar. This type of stimulation is called enrichment and is critical to preventing boredom and depression in animals in captivity.

THE WALKING COCONUT: TOOL USE

In some parts of Southeast Asia, people grow and process coconuts for their oil and sweet, meaty flesh, and the husks can end up in the ocean.

A veined octopus hides out in a coconut shell in ocean waters off the island nation of Indonesia. Look for amazing online videos of octopuses getting creative with coconut shells by searching for "octopus coconut shell."

One day in 1999, Julian Finn, an Australian marine biologist, was diving off the coast of northern Sulawesi, an island in Indonesia, when he spotted something unusual. A coconut husk on the seafloor was moving. As Finn looked closer, he realized a veined octopus was underneath the coconut shell.

As Finn watched, the octopus flipped the coconut shell over, dome side up, straddled it with all eight legs and scooted across the ocean floor in a "stilt walk," moving forward on the tips of its many arms. Finn recalled the sight as "extremely comical."

So far, the veined octopus is the only marine animal known to use coconut shells in this way, but it wasn't the first time tool use had been recorded in an octopus. Jennifer Mather of Canada's University of Lethbridge had observed octopuses building walls outside their dens, perhaps to keep out predators. With Mark Norman, another Australian marine biologist, Finn later observed more octopuses carrying around coconut shells.

THE MIMIC OCTOPUS
(*THAUMOCTOPUS MIMICUS*)

Fishermen first discovered the mimic octopus off the coast of Sulawesi in Indonesia in 1998. Like most other octopuses, this quick-change artist uses chromatophore cells in its skin to change its color and texture. Scientists believe this camouflage is a form of protection against predators. It is also a sign of intelligence.

Most octopuses and their relatives the cuttlefish use their chromatophores to blend into their environment. They are adept at blending into rocks, sponges, and corals. Yet unlike other octopuses, *Thaumoctopus* can also mimic the shapes and movements of various venomous predators as yet another form of protection. Some animals have mimicry built into their bodies. But the mimic octopus is the only animal known to choose what to mimic, depending on the situation.

What's in the mimic octopus repertoire? Mostly, they mimic venomous animals such as jellyfish and sea snakes. And mimic octopuses appear to tailor their mimicry to individual threats, another sign of intelligence. For instance, when attacked by damselfishes, *Thaumoctopus* imitates the sea snake, which preys on damselfishes.

To ward off an attack by a damselfish, this *Thaumoctopus mimicus* perfectly mimics the black-and-white striping pattern of a sea snake, the damselfish's predator.

Through observation Norman and Finn eventually realized that octopuses look for more than one coconut shell. They stack them one on top of the other, and when threatened by a predator, they drop the shell, scoot inside, and close the halves around their bodies as a protective shelter.

Finn says that preparing protective cover before it's actually needed is "like us carrying an umbrella around in case it rains." And assembling the coconut shells to build a shelter is a behavior that animal behaviorists refer to as tool use. Both anticipation of need and tool use are key signs of sophisticated animal intelligence.

When You Give an Octopus Some LEGO: Play

We've all seen the videos: an elephant calf cavorting in a kiddie pool, meerkats wrestling, and young foxes bouncing on a backyard trampoline. Young animals, especially mammals, seem to take joy in playing. But what about invertebrates? Do they play?

A team of scientists at the Konrad Lorenz Institute for Evolution and Cognition Research in Austria wanted to investigate the question, and they settled on octopuses for their experiment. The experiments were conducted between December 2002 and September 2003. They gave the fourteen octopuses in their study LEGO bricks and food items.

"Filming and later watching over seven hundred hours of octopuses interacting (more or less) with the LEGO requires more than just patience—you need determination and the wish to see and document something no one else has before," experimenter Michael Kuba said. "The work could be funny, like when I would try to remove the objects from an octopus's grasp and we would play tug-of-war for up to fifteen minutes. And octopuses will squirt water at you to make you go away—and they are very good at aiming for your face. More than once I went home wet."

Kuba and his team filmed the octopuses with the LEGOs and the food, ranking their behaviors on a scale of 0 to 4. The low end of the scale indicated instinctive or reflex behavior, while the higher end of the scale reflected sophisticated intelligence. Because an octopus will explore anything introduced into its tank, team members ranked the animal holding an object close to its mouth as a 0. If the octopus explored the

It turns out that many octopuses love to play with LEGO toys. In one study, the octopuses towed them, pushed and pulled them, and passed them from arm to arm to arm to arm. In fact, some of the octopuses were reluctant to give up their LEGOs. This advanced play behavior is a key sign of intelligence.

LEGO with its arms, the team gave this behavior a score of 1. If the octopus briefly towed the LEGO in one direction, pushed or pulled it or passed it between a few arms, the team gave it a score of 2.

The team noticed, however, that ten of the fourteen octopuses in the test were much more playful. They towed the LEGO back and forth. They pushed and pulled it over and over. They passed it from arm to arm to arm to arm to arm. For brief playlike behavior, the experimenters assigned a score of 3. In one of the octopuses, however, the playlike behavior lasted longer than in the other animals. The experimenters described that behavior as play and rated it a 4.

Why would octopuses play in the wild? Marine biologists who study behavior have some theories about that. Some researchers think play emerges when animals have plenty of resources, such as food, territory, and mates. In this surplus resource theory, animals are not spending all their time meeting basic needs, so they have time on their arms, flippers, hooves, or paws. They fill this time with what looks to us as play behavior. Other researchers hypothesize that play is training for the unexpected. Like mammals, octopuses live in a fast-changing environment. Playing may make them nimble at adapting to new conditions. The late Roland Anderson, a biologist who had worked with octopuses at the Seattle Aquarium, said "Only intelligent animals play."

Touchy-Feely: Octopus Personality

Octopuses exhibit a range of behaviors that suggest high intelligence. Animal behaviorists also suspect that octopuses have personalities. Researcher Jennifer Mather had heard anecdotes of shy, touchy-feely, and downright destructive octopuses. She wanted to know more about octopus personality, so with her colleague Roland Anderson, Mather designed an experiment, the first ever to document invertebrate personality.

In the three-year study in the early 1990s, Mather and Anderson tested the personalities of forty-four octopuses that had been born in the wild. They recorded how each octopus reacted to three conditions: when the lid of its tank was lifted, when the animal was touched with a brush for cleaning test tubes, and when a live crab was dropped into the tank. The investigators called these three conditions alerting, threat, and feeding. Each octopus went through seven trials, or sessions, of these three conditions and received a score for the presence of nineteen possible behaviors.

The test tube brush caused the widest array of differing reactions among the octopuses. Facing this strange, new object, some of the animals fled to a corner of the tank or disappeared into the safety of their dens, usually a small flowerpot. Others released a cloud of ink, a protective behavior to hide themselves from view while making an escape. By contrast, others reached out with a tentacle, grabbed the brush, and pulled.

After analyzing the wealth of data, the researchers concluded that octopus personality varied along three scales: bold-to-shy, reactive-to-calm, and active-to-inactive. Yet despite the amazing results of this experiment, Mather notes that people tend to reject the idea that animals have personalities, and additional experiments are under way to learn more about animal personality. Many, if not most, pet owners will easily accept that the family dog has a personality, however. Mather says, "Of course dogs have personalities, but then why wouldn't octopuses have them, too? Both species are smart, adaptable, learning and coping with different situations." She believes too that personality in the animal kingdom is an adaptive behavior necessary for survival. "Personalities help octopuses fit into part of the big, variable environment," she says, "so of course they have [personalities]."

CHAPTER FOUR

HONEY BEES
AND
PAPER WASPS

Honey bees live in hive colonies with complex social structures. Scientists have observed that the bees display sophisticated patterns of communication to share information with the other bees in their colony. This is a sign of intelligence.

MEET THE HONEY BEE

COMMON NAMES: It is called the European honey bee or the Western honey bee.

NICKNAME: Its nickname is honey bee.

WHAT SCIENTISTS CALL IT: *Apis mellifera* (*A. mellifera*)

RELATIVES: The genus *Apis* has at least seven species of honey bee.

HOW BIG IS IT? The worker bee is up to 6/10 inch (15 mm) long. The queen, at up to 8/10 inch (20 mm), is much larger.

WHERE'S HOME? Honey bees originated in Europe, western Asia, and Africa and were carried to North America by Europeans in the 1600s. Because humans are fond of honey, honey bees are found almost anywhere that flowers bloom.

FAVORITE FOODS: Bees eat nectar and pollen from many kinds of flowering plants. In winter, bees eat the honey they make and store in their hives.

KNOWN FOR: It is known for being busy, working hard, and turning flower nectar into honey.

BRAIN SIZE: The brain size is 0.00006 inches (1 cu. mm). You could fit one million honey bee brains in a quart-sized (one-liter) soda bottle. Each honey bee brain is packed with 960,000 neurons.

Biologist Tom Seeley of Cornell University applies tiny license plates to the backs of honey bees. On the thorax, to be exact. But first, he has to lower the bee's body temperature so it won't sting him. In a lab refrigerator, he chills ten to fifteen bees at a time in a plastic freezer bag. Because the group of bees is small, they can't huddle together for warmth. Soon all the bees enter a chill coma. Then Seeley and his team of labelers glue a plastic tag to each thorax and apply a dab of paint to each bee's abdomen. The tags come in five different colors, numbered 0 to 99. The abdomen paint comes in eight colors. This gives Seeley four thousand unique combinations of tag color, tag number, and abdomen paint. That's the size of the artificial swarm he creates to study how honey bees look for and decide on a location for their colony's new hive site, a process biologists call house hunting.

The bees in honey bee colonies have different roles and are in different life stages. The resident bees of any hive include larvae (immature bees), worker bees (some have nursery duty, others are foragers, some repair the

HONEYBEE VS. HONEY BEE

Entomologists (biologists who study insects) do not spell the name of bees as one word. Instead, they prefer two words, such as honey bee, as well as bumble bee, sweat bee, miner bee, and paper wasp. Compounds are reserved for yellowjackets, dragonflies, and butterflies. Entomologists prefer the single words because yellowjackets aren't jackets and dragonflies and butterflies aren't flies.

hive, and others take care of the queen), and a queen bee (who lays eggs). The drones (males) travel from hive to hive, mating with the queens. Each colony's hive is also filled with honey. When the hive gets overcrowded, it will do what beekeepers call casting a swarm. In this situation, about ten thousand bees leave the hive with the original queen, often gathering nearby in a single mass on a tree branch.

For decades, Seeley and his students and colleagues have been investigating just how bees decide among multiple real estate options. The scientists focus their attention on how bee colonies are organized. For example, according to Seeley, many people falsely assume that a queen bee is a sort of Royal Decider. Seeley says that's not the case at all. Rather, she is the Royal Egg Layer, laying fifteen hundred eggs a day—just under one a minute. All the worker bees in the colony are her daughters. The queen,

HONEY BEES IN PERIL

Honey bee swarms are harmless to humans so you should never interfere with one because you might harm the bees. They will eventually fly off to their new home. However, because people—especially those with allergies to beestings—fear large masses of bees, countless swarms are killed unnecessarily each year across the world. Honey bees are critical pollinators, but their population worldwide is in rapid decline, due to parasitic varroa mites that spread viruses to honey bee colonies. Toxic pesticides are a threat too. A class of pesticides called neonicotinoids has been linked to Colony Collapse Disorder, a situation in which all the bees of a colony disappear.

Scientists and beekeepers urge people to do whatever they can to promote honey bee survival by planting flowers that attract the bees, avoiding the use of pesticides, or building bee houses for native bees. For more ideas about how to help bees, visit www.buzzaboutbees.net.

however, doesn't tell them what to do.

To look for potential nest sites, female bees known as scout bees go house hunting. They come back to the swarm to campaign for their site. After a form of honey-bee debate in which a new site is chosen, the swarm rises up into the air and takes off for the new nest site. The swarm almost always decides on an excellent nest site. Such sites are in a safe, shaded cavity of a tree or in a cavity that has a small entrance, one that can be easily defended against predators. How do they pull off this feat?

SCOUTS SCOUR THE COUNTRYSIDE

As soon as a colony casts a swarm, the swarm will settle near the original hive, often hanging from the branch of a tree, while the scouts go off house hunting. Hundreds of scouts comb up to 30 square miles (78 square kilometers) for possible nest sites.

When a beehive becomes overpopulated, the bees will cast a swarm (above), collecting in large numbers on a nearby tree branch. Such swarms are not dangerous to humans. The bees will eventually find a new home that can accommodate the larger number of bees.

When an individual scout bee discovers a potential site, she spends fifteen minutes to an hour carefully examining it. She walks up to 200 feet (61 m) inside the cavity, carefully inspecting every surface and measuring the volume of the nest site. Cavities need to be large enough to hold enough honey to last the colony through the winter. If the nest site isn't big enough,

Honey bees communicate information to one another about sources of water, flowers, and new nesting sites through a movement known as the waggle dance *(above)*. The dance involves multiple passes through a small figure-eight pattern. The direction and duration of the passes through the dance indicate the direction and the distance of the water, flowers, or nesting site.

the colony will starve. Drafty or damp nest sites can be repaired. Bees aren't afraid of a fixer-upper. But they prefer a nest site with a small entrance that is easier for the colony to defend.

CAMPAIGNING BEGINS

Seeley's research has shown that the scouts come back to the swarm and do a waggle dance to tell their sisters about different nest sites. Each scout's dance contains a lot of information about a potential nest site: its direction relative to the sun and its distance from the swarm, the direction of a resource (whether the resource is a new nest site or a nectar-rich patch of flowers), the distance to the resource, and the quality of the resource. Bees

MEMORY BOOST FROM CAFFEINE

The nectar of flowers of the coffee plant and of certain citrus trees contains trace amounts of caffeine. Scientific experiments have shown that bees who sipped caffeine nectar were more likely to remember the scent of the coffee plant's flowers and to remember the reward (nectar) longer. In evolutionary terms, by ensuring that bees remember the sweet reward, the coffee plant may be guaranteeing that bees regularly visit the plant to carry its pollen to another coffee plant and thereby promote the plant's survival.

known as recruits learn these directions from the scouts and fly off to check out the different sites for themselves. If they approve of a site, they will come back and dance for it too. Seeley and his students learned that the more high quality the nest site, the more vigorous the dance. "All this [scout bees dancing on the swarm] makes the surface of a swarm look at first like a riotous dance party," Seeley says.

A Decision Is Made

How is a decision made? Scouts and recruits each dance for their own site. Long, strong dances win out over short, weak dances to convince the other bees, and gradually they are all dancing for the same site. Seeley's research has revealed that honey bees have a kind of democracy. The site with the most votes (dances) wins. Tom Seeley thinks honey bees have a kind of collective intelligence. He calls it the wisdom of the hive.

Moving Day

Before the swarm can take off for the new nest site, the bees have to warm up for flight. Scouts stop dancing and begin to pipe a special signal that means "warm up." Seeley says it sounds kind of like a race car speeding down a track. They then grab individual worker bees and shake them to warm them up. Once every bee is warm enough to take flight, the scouts begin performing buzz runs, bulldozing through their warm nestmates, telling them to launch into flight. Finally, the whole swarm lifts off and flies off to the newly chosen nest site.

MEET THE NORTHERN PAPER WASP

COMMON NAMES: It is called the northern paper wasp or the golden paper wasp.

NICKNAME: Its nickname is paper wasp.

WHAT SCIENTISTS CALL IT: *Polistes fuscatus* (*P. fuscatus*)

RELATIVES: At least three hundred different species of paper wasps make up the global population of this insect.

HOW BIG IS IT? Workers are 6/10 inch (15 mm) long. Queens are about 8/10 inch (20 mm) long.

WHERE'S HOME? North America

FAVORITE FOODS: Adult wasps live on plant nectar, and they feed insect prey such as caterpillars to developing wasp larvae.

KNOWN FOR: Being insect architects. These wasps chew up wood to make a gray pulp, which they form into a soccer-ball-sized, chambered nest.

BRAIN SIZE: Workers of a related species, *P. instabilis*, have a brain volume of 0.00003 cubic inches (0.525 cu. mm), according to Sean O'Donnell of Drexel University in Philadelphia, Pennsylvania.

Polistes fuscatus (northern paper wasp)

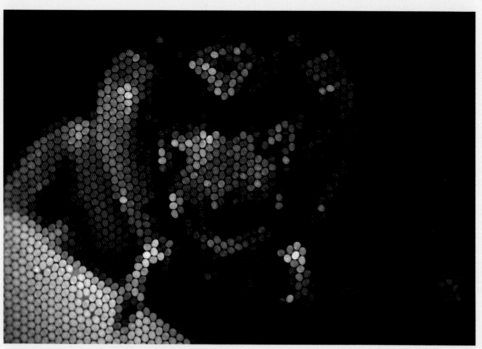

This image captures how a northern paper wasp would perceive the face of another northern paper wasp. These wasps have the best memory of any insect, and they have an especially good memory for wasp faces. Memory is a major indicator of intelligence.

FRIEND OR FOE?

House-hunting behavior in honey bees is one indicator of invertebrate intelligence among Hymenoptera, the insect order to which ants, bees, wasps, and sawflies belong. In an intelligence experiment in the early 2000s with graduate student Michael Sheehan at the University of Michigan, evolutionary biologist Elizabeth Tibbetts had shown that northern paper wasps, or *Polistes fuscatus* (*P. fuscatus*) have good memories for faces. In fact, they have the best memory of any insect yet tested, and memory is a key indicator of animal intelligence. Tibbetts and Sheehan then began to wonder whether wasps, with their tiny brains, could identify individual nestmates and whether they were any better at memorizing faces than other kinds of images, such as abstract symbols or pictures of caterpillars, a favorite food. So they created an experiment to study recognition skills among two different species of wasps—the northern paper wasp and the metricus paper wasp, or *Polistes metricus* (*P. metricus*).

Because northern paper wasps have more than one queen, their colonies are organized according to strict social rules. *Metricus* paper wasps, on the other hand, have only a single queen, with a less strict social hierarchy. With this information in mind, Tibbetts and Sheehan designed their recognition experiment. For both types of wasps, a simple T-shaped maze offered the insects two choices. One arm of the maze was set up with a face of a wasp stranger. That arm led to a mild electric shock not strong enough to hurt the wasp but strong enough to be unpleasant. The other arm of the maze had a face of a wasp nestmate. That arm led to a safety zone without a shock.

Sheehan and Tibbetts found that the northern paper wasp, the species with a strict social hierarchy, was better at recognizing wasp faces than abstract symbols or pictures of caterpillars. It was also capable of learning that the foe wasp face (the stranger) led to the shock and that the friend wasp face (the nestmate) led to the safety zone. In contrast, *P. metricus* wasps repeatedly failed to learn to associate the face of the foe wasp with the electric shock.

This makes sense in light of what Tibbetts and Sheehan already knew about the way these wasps live. In *Polistes fuscatus* colonies, more than one queen will establish a nest in spring, but only the alpha, or highest-ranking, queen will lay eggs. Through bouts of aggressive behavior, the sister queens determine a hierarchical pecking order below the alpha queen. The sister queens are able to recognize other wasp faces, and through these visual cues, they know when they are outranked and avoid fighting with wasps that are higher in the social order of the hive. *P. metricus* has only a single queen, however, so fighting over rank is not likely in these hives and a strict hierarchy is therefore not observed. Biologists believe that because these wasps have no real need to observe rank, facial recognition is not critical to survival in the *P. metricus* world. For that reason, the species has limited facial recognition skills.

BLACK BELTS FOR PAPER WASPS

The European paper wasp (*Polistes dominula*) functions as a fighter in a way similar to that of a karate practitioner of black belt status, says evolutionary biologist Elizabeth Tibbetts. Some wasps emerge from their pupation (the third life stage of some types of insects) with more spots than other wasps at the same stage. The more spots a fighter has, the more expert she appears to be at defending her territory.

Tibbetts wanted to learn more about how the wasps are able to distinguish good fighters from weak fighters. She took paper wasp queens that she had observed to be poor fighters in the fighting arena and painted their faces with ink spots to make them look like they had the wasp equivalent of a black belt in karate. As a control group, for comparative purposes, she also painted the faces of other wasps that were poor fighters but without altering the pattern to make them look like black belts.

The expert fighters weren't fooled. In videotaped bouts between two queens, the expert fighters beat up the pretenders, biting them, grappling with them, and climbing on top of them to show dominance.

European paper wasps are black, with yellow markings on their faces and yellow stripes on their bodies. The black spots on their faces *(right)* indicate gender and social status. Additionally, the more spots a queen wasp has, the more aggressive she is in her fighting behavior. This series of images shows a range of spotting and facial markings.

CHAPTER FIVE

ARGENTINE ANTS

Argentine ants *(above)*, like other ants, are social insects that live in enormous colonies. They display a type of intelligence that scientists refer to as collective, or swarm, intelligence. This type of intelligence allows the entire community of ants to act as one organism, in which each of the ants follows a few collectively understood rules.

MEET THE ARGENTINE ANT

COMMON NAMES: In its native Argentina, this ant is known as the sugar ant. Everywhere else it's known as the Argentine ant.

NICKNAMES: None

WHAT SCIENTISTS CALL IT: *Linepithema humile (L. humile)*

RELATIVES: Argentine ants belong to a subfamily of ants called the Dolichoderinae, or the odorous ants. These ants don't sting, but they do stink bomb their enemies, releasing foul-smelling chemicals to ward off predators or rival ants.

HOW BIG IS IT? It is a little longer than ⅛ inch (3.2 mm).

WHERE'S HOME? Originally from northern Argentina, this invasive insect has spread through the Mediterranean region of southern Europe and into parts of Australia and New Zealand, parts of Japan, South Africa, and even to some Pacific islands. The ants are particularly at home in places with a Mediterranean climate—not too wet or dry. They don't like rain forests or deserts.

FAVORITE FOODS: This omnivorous ant will eat anything.

KNOWN FOR: It is known for taking over the world, except Antarctica and the Arctic.

BRAIN SIZE: No one has measured the Argentine ant brain, but Neil Tsutsui, an evolutionary biologist at the University of California, Berkeley, estimates it may be the same size as a fruit fly brain, about one hundred thousand neurons.

Sometime before 1890, a ship from Brazil bearing sacks of either coffee or sugar (historians aren't sure) arrived in the port of New Orleans, Louisiana. In its cargo, the ship was carrying tiny stowaways: the Argentine ant, *Linepithema humile*. Some of those ants escaped, and by 1907, the Argentine ant had set tarsus (or foot) in California. Historians of science speculate the ants may have hitched a ride out west on a freight train. Within a few years, those original ants had formed a supercolony. By the twenty-first century, the Large Supercolony, as it is known, stretches for more than 600 miles (966 km) along the California coast, from San Francisco to northern Mexico. Ant researcher and explorer Mark W. Moffett of the Smithsonian Institution estimates the Large Supercolony may be home to as many as one trillion ants.

Think that's weird?
Well, ant researchers have
determined that the Large
Supercolony is part of an
even larger megacolony that
also includes ants on the
other side of the Atlantic and
Pacific Oceans. If you were
to drop ants from the Large
Supercolony in California into
a nest of Argentine ants in
Japan or into a nest along the
coast of the Mediterranean
Sea in Europe, the residents of
those colonies would not attack
the newcomers as strangers.

Ants communicate through scented chemicals called
pheromones. Ants use the tips of their antennae to smell
the pheromones, of which there are about ten to twenty
types that all ants in the colony recognize. Chemically
communicated messages tell the other ants many things,
including where food is or that it's time to attack prey or
to defend the colony.

All ants use chemical communication—smell—to tell friend from foe. As
long as the new ants smell right, the others accept them as colony mates.
Moffett says that "the [Argentine] ants' aggressive response to each other's
body smell acts like an immune system—killing all outsiders . . . no matter
how big the colony grows."

In an ant subdivision outside San Diego, California, however, it's all-out
war. Here is where the border of the Large Supercolony meets the borders
of three other ant supercolonies. Melissa Thomas, an evolutionary biologist
and ant researcher at the University of Western Australia, has estimated
that as many as fifteen million ants die in skirmishes along this border in a
six-month period.

How do such megacolonies form, and what makes them work? To
understand the Argentine ant, you must first understand the sugar ant back
home in Argentina.

A.K.A. THE SUGAR ANT

Home is the flood plain of the Paraná River, which flows through
woodlands in Brazil, Paraguay, and Argentina. In this region of South

America, Argentine ants are known as sugar ants and their colonies are small. The sugar ants are extremely territorial. If you carry an ant from one sugar ant nest to a nearby field and drop it into a different sugar ant nest, the ants in the second nest will kill it.

Frequent seasonal floods have turned these ants into warriors. Every time the Paraná overflows its banks, sugar ants climb to higher ground, even into the treetops, to escape drowning. When the waters recede, the ants must fight to establish the colony's territory all over again. Over thousands of generations, repeated territorial battles have shaped the sugar ant into a lean, mean fighting machine.

Scientists speculate that because these ants are pushed around by floodwaters so much, they are nomads, moving their nests to different spots. They aren't fussy about where they live. Under a rock and a leaf will do, though they may move several times during the course of a single day. They aren't picky eaters, either. While they prefer sugary honeydew—a secretion that aphids leave behind on plants—the sugar ants are among the most omnivorous of all ants, eating flower nectar and even other insects.

In the Paraná flood plain, other native Argentine ant species are the natural predators that keep the population of the sugar ant in check. But native ants of North America, Europe, and Asia aren't able to defeat the tiny sugar ants. In the United States, they have no natural predators, so their colonies become enormously big. Argentine ant workers—the ones who bring food back to the nest—are able to outcompete native ants for food sources. And in large groups, the Argentine ants tackle and overwhelm much bigger ants that invade their territory, tearing them limb from limb from limb. Because the Argentine ants are so aggressive, they dominate the ant world no matter which continent they call home.

THE COLONY AS "SUPERORGANISM"

The most well-studied social insects (those that live in colonies) are ants, bees, termites, and wasps. Bert Hölldobler of Arizona State University and E. O. Wilson of Harvard University are experts on the lives of social insects. They study how social-insect colonies function as superorganisms.

These large units of animals are made up of individuals that have highly specialized divisions of labor, work cooperatively, and can only survive as part of the larger unit. Deborah Gordon of Stanford University in California says, "A colony is [similar] to a brain where there are a lot of neurons, each of which can only do something very simple, but together the whole brain can think. None of the [individual] neurons [ants] can think ant, but the brain [as a whole] can think ant."

Most insect societies rely on a caste (hierarchical, or rank) system for division of labor. Ants live in colonies, and each colony has a queen. Once the queen mates, she spends the rest of her life laying eggs. The rest of the colony is populated by worker ants, who are all female. Some ant and termite species have a soldier caste. Those female ants do the heavy lifting for the colony and are the first on the battle lines when conflict erupts.

Among social insects, more than one generation of adults shares a nest. The new generation doesn't go out to found a colony of its own. Instead, the new-generation worker ants stay in the nest in which they were born, raising the newest brood (larvae), bringing food back to the nest, cleaning and feeding the queen, and defending the nest from attack. Instead of mating and laying eggs themselves, worker ants raise their sisters.

COLLECTIVE INTELLIGENCE

All social insect colonies, including those of the Argentine ant, represent a collective intelligence. The decision-making process is decentralized, which means that no one ant, bee, wasp, or termite is smart or in charge of its colony mates. Not even the queen is in charge. Instead, the entire colony acts as a single superorganism in which its members all obey a few dozen rules. Ants and other social insects are born knowing the rules for their caste. The rules are in the deoxyribonucleic acid (DNA) that makes up their genetic code.

Scientists observe group intelligence, sometimes referred to as swarm intelligence, in a wide range of animals from social insects to naked mole rats to crows and dolphins. Group intelligence is characteristic of hierarchical societies with castes (ranks) to carry out the division of labor that ensures the colony's survival.

COPYING ANT DECISION MAKING

Ant collective intelligence is something that a variety of human researchers are investigating for high-tech applications. For example, software engineers are interested in how ants and other social insects carry out their collective intelligence. Using mathematical equations called algorithms, writers of computer code are using the science of swarms to allow the software that supports the Internet to deliver packets of data faster. Improved software will also be key to designing more efficient delivery routes to help companies get their products to customers more quickly. In Switzerland, for example, a company called AntOptima is putting ant swarm algorithms to work to manage high-efficiency delivery of everything from groceries to gasoline.

Robot engineers are also very interested in swarming behavior. They have created tiny robot swarms, or swarmbots. At Harvard University's Self-Organizing Systems Research Group, headed up by engineer Radhika Nagpal, the team has designed and built kilobots. These collectives include hundreds, even thousands, of tiny robots, each about the size of a US quarter and perched on three legs. Inspired by social insects, these kilobot swarms are decentralized—like ants, no single kilobot is in charge. Using infrared light, engineers send programming code to the kilobots, telling them to Run Program. The researchers use the kilobots for educational purposes and to research how swarms work. In the future, the kilobots might be able to scan the environment for pollutants, help bees pollinate crops, or seek out survivors buried in rubble.

Elsewhere at Harvard University, in the Microrobotics Lab, Robert Wood is designing robots based on bees. The robobees are lightweight and made of soft materials. He envisions that one day they will explore situations and places unsafe

for humans: search and rescue efforts, toxic environments, and outer space. And the robobees are also great at getting students excited about robotics!

Researchers at Harvard University have created robotic swarms *(left)* to learn more about collective intelligence and how it works.

CHAPTER SIX

MANTIS SHRIMPS

A peacock mantis shrimp uses the force and velocity of its powerful dactyl club to smash the shell of its snail prey. Mantis shrimp are fearsome—and intelligent—invertebrates. They have complex forms of communication, are capable of learning, can retrieve memories of previous encounters, and can adjust their strategies when fighting with other shrimps.

MEET THE PEACOCK MANTIS SHRIMP

COMMON NAMES: It is called harlequin mantis shrimp or painted mantis shrimp.

NICKNAME: None

WHAT SCIENTISTS CALL IT: *Odontodactylus scyllarus* (*O. scyllarus*)

RELATIVES: More than five hundred species of mantis shrimps are known to live around the world.

HOW BIG IS IT? Peacock mantis shrimps are about 7 inches (18 cm) long.

WHERE'S HOME? It lives in coral reefs, sea grass beds, and sand flats of coastal areas.

FAVORITE FOODS: It eats snails, clams, and crabs.

KNOWN FOR: It is known for striking with five hundred newtons of force and with the same acceleration as a .22-caliber bullet. This is enough force to break aquarium glass.

BRAIN SIZE: It has not yet been measured.

The snail doesn't realize it yet, but it's doomed. Hidden in its burrow of coral rubble in the sea, a peacock mantis shrimp has sensed the snail's presence, using its remarkable eyes and the chemical sensors on its antennae. The mantis shrimp shoots out of its burrow, using a hammerlike appendage called a dactyl club to hit the snail on its shell. The strike is so fast that it occurs in less than two thousandths of a second. The acceleration of the dactyl club has been compared to that of a bullet fired from a .22-caliber handgun. The strike is so rapid that the water at the point of impact actually vaporizes, a process known as cavitation. The cavitation shock wave can stun and even kill the unlucky snail. Then the peacock mantis shrimp hammers away at the snail's shell until it breaks, dining on the soft interior flesh of the snail.

Peacock mantis shrimps—along with other mantis shrimps—are a top invertebrate predator in coral reefs, sea grass beds, and sand flats of coastal areas. But mantis shrimps aren't mantises and they aren't shrimps. They are more properly known as stomatopods, a type of crustacean, an aquatic animal with an exoskeleton. Most stomatopods are between 2 and 7 inches long (5 and 18 cm), and they look like tiny lobsters. Some stomatopods are smashers, specializing in targeting hard-shelled prey.

MEET NINJABOT

Doctoral candidate Suzanne Cox of the University of Massachusetts Amherst has built a Ninjabot to model the mantis shrimp's speedy strike. This underwater robot allows Cox to break down the mantis shrimp strike into phases and allows her to measure each phase precisely. Creating Ninjabot was a challenge. Cox explains her work and her amazement at the mantis shrimp and its skills:

> When [biologist] Sheila Patek first pitched the idea [of Ninjabot] to members of the mechanical engineering department, they said it couldn't be done. It required too much force in too small a mechanism. But of course it had been done: by the mantis shrimp.
>
> The hard part was making Ninjabot reusable, safe, and adjustable and doing it all in salt water. Regular bearings don't work underwater. The drag [resistance] at [the mantis shrimp's quick] accelerations is astounding. So not only do you need to generate the forces necessary to accelerate a body that fast, but you need to overcome the resulting drag. That magnifies the forces involved and they were so great that my first generation of Ninjabot bent its own frame every time it struck. So, once you generate enough force, how do you make [the arm] rotate smoothly and not slow down just due to friction? The whole process made me marvel at the mantis shrimp. In the end it took almost twenty pounds [9 kg] of stainless steel for Ninjabot to approximate what the mantis shrimp does with [about] 0.4 grams [0.01 ounces] of exoskeleton and muscle.

Cox has adapted Ninjabot's strike capacity so she can see what effect different strikes have. Ninjabot even creates a cavitation shock wave. But it's still not as fast as the fastest mantis shrimp.

Ninjabot is a mechanical model that can almost replicate the mantis shrimp strike. It weighs about 20 pounds (9 kg), far more than the shrimp itself, and can't yet strike as quickly as the invertebrate can. All the same, it is a useful tool for scientists to learn more about the shrimp's strike capacity. The part labeled "a" in this image is the equivalent of the animal's dactyl club.

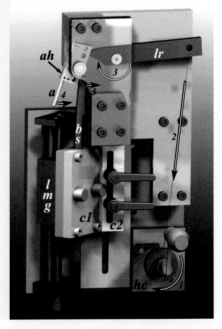

Others are spearers, hiding in the sand, using their own dactyl claws, which are modified into spears to stab small fish and other prey.

The Mechanics of Movement

Sheila Patek at Duke University in North Carolina is studying the physics of the mantis shrimp strike. She and the members of her lab want to learn what the secret to its spring mechanism is and exactly how the dactyl club moves as the mantis shrimp uses it. How does the mantis shrimp, with its small body, manage the fastest strike in the ocean? How did the dactyl club evolve and how does it amplify its power?

Patek says the mantis's strike capability may be similar to that of a person using a crossbow. With this weapon, someone must contract arm muscles to load the bow and to press the latch that releases the arrow. The arrow flies through the air at far greater speeds than would have been possible had the person simply thrown the arrow. The technical term for this process is power amplification, and Patek believes mantis shrimps and trap-jaw ants may have similar capabilities in their appendages.

Mantis Shrimp Vision

Once a peacock mantis shrimp has identified a potential prey animal or predator, it must strike quickly and accurately. If the animal's aim is off or if it misses, the club can be damaged and therefore useless for feeding and self-defense. Scientific research has shown that the mantis shrimp relies on its keen senses, especially its vision, to estimate distance and to make decisions about how and when to strike.

Stomatopods have eyes on stalks that protrude from the head. The stalks allow them to size up predators, prey, and even other mantis shrimp from the safety of their coral burrows. In 1984 British neuroscientist Michael F. Land called stomatopods "crustacean primates." Land is now an emeritus professor at the University of Sussex in England. He explains what he meant:

> Stomatopods look around with their eyes in an apparently
> intelligent and curiously primate-like way. When you look closely,
> however you find that the two eyes are usually not looking in the

The two eyes *(top)* of a peacock mantis shrimp are on stalks at the front of the body. Each stalk can move independently. Among other things, the shrimp's complex vision allows the invertebrate to recognize different types of coral, prey, and predators and provides precise depth perception.

same direction, and stranger still they rotate in different directions. They do this to scan the scene for color and polarization [light waves in which the vibrations occur in a single plane], but this procedure makes them seem quite alien, and unlike any other animal.

The eyes of some mantis shrimps have three zones. The upper and lower parts of their eyes detect motion and polarized light. A strip in the middle detects color down into the ultraviolet spectrum (the range of the light spectrum that is not visible to human eyes). The mantis shrimps can have up to twelve kinds of light-sensing cells in their eyes, far more than what is necessary among invertebrates and vertebrates for even extreme color vision. Recent work by Justin Marshall and his students at the University of Queensland in Australia showed that mantis shrimps aren't that good at telling colors apart, however. Mantis shrimps seem to scan objects using all twelve kinds of light-sensing cells at once.

A BrilLiant Mistake

Mantis shrimps have impressive hunting skills, and they appear to have complex systems of communication as well. At the beginning of his career as a biologist in the 1970s, Roy Caldwell of the University of California, Berkeley, was studying mantis shrimps to learn more about how stomatopod males communicate with one another. He decided to stage a tournament in which each of sixteen combatants would fight one another over the course of fifteen days. Caldwell wanted to see how rival males decided who was dominant. Mantis shrimps are highly aggressive, and after posturing and sizing each other up, they wrestle until one stomatopod emerges victorious. These fights can last up to five minutes, which is a long time in the stomatopod world.

Then Caldwell made a brilliant mistake. Because of an error in his record keeping, he accidentally paired mantis shrimps that had already battled. When facing a rematch, the loser immediately fled from the shrimp who had won in the previous match. Caldwell wondered if the losing mantis shrimp somehow recognized the winning mantis shrimp, and if so, how?

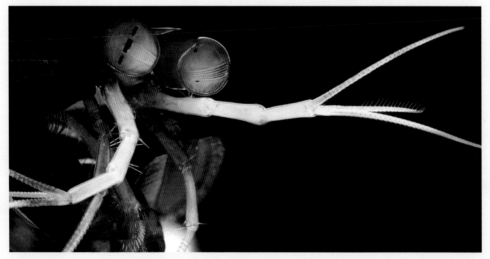

Mantis shrimps rely on sensory hairs *(above, far right)* on their antennules (small antennae) to identify the odor of other stomatopods.

"Over the course of the next several years, a few thousand cuticle-bruising fights later, I eventually could say with some certainty that mantis shrimps were capable of identifying individuals they had previously fought, and adjusting their fight strategy accordingly," Caldwell remembers.

In the late 1990s, physiologist Kristina M. Vetter, then at Berkeley in the lab of biologist Mimi Koehl, discovered that mantis shrimps detect dissolved chemicals in seawater through chemical sensors lodged in hairs on their bodies. In separate research, Caldwell showed that mantis shrimps use these same sensors to identify individuals against which they've fought, as well as to identify potential mates, prey, and predators.

Mantis Shrimp ChatTer

Scientists have discovered that mantis shrimps have other forms of communication as well. For example, Caldwell thinks mantis shrimps flash scales of their antennae at one another as one way to communicate. Because mantis shrimps are biofluorescent—absorbing light energy and returning it to the surroundings as lower-energy light—scientists can only see the flashes with cameras equipped with yellow filters. Other shrimps can see the fluorescent flashes, which generally communicate information about mantis shrimp territory and who has the right to a particular den.

MANTIS SHRIMP CAN SEE CANCER...

. . . thanks to the way they see polarized light. Researchers are using a camera based on stomatopods' eyes to improve polarized cameras already in use for cancer detection. Scientists know that cancerous tissue tends to reflect light differently than healthy tissue. Humans can't see polarized light. For this reason, researchers use a camera that converts polarized light into colors that the human eye can see, as one way to determine if a tissue sample contains cancerous cells. This noninvasive method may reduce the need for biopsies and exploratory surgeries, though not the need for surgery to remove the tumor. Neurobiology professor Justin Marshall of the University of Queensland in Australia says, "Nature has come up with elegant and efficient design principles, so we are combining the mantis shrimp's millions of years of evolution—nature's engineering—with our relatively few years of work with the [camera] technology."

One species of mantis shrimps—*Hemisquilla californiensis*—also communicate with low rumbles. These shrimp have a kind of chorus at dawn and dusk where many mantis shrimps join in. Eventually they all chorus together like frogs in a pond. These shrimp may be communicating with potential mates or defending their territories.

Learning and Other Signs of Intelligence

Another feature of mantis shrimp intelligence is the crustacean's capacity for using its maxillipeds (food-handling appendages) to construct burrows, to handle prey, and during mating and fights with other mantis shrimps. More significantly, mantis shrimps show a capacity for learning—a key component of intelligence. For example, mantis shrimps can learn the chemical signature of various predators. In the wild, the Caribbean rock mantis shrimp coexists with an Atlantic pygmy octopus. In one study, stomatopods who had previously encountered a pygmy octopus "smelled" octopus odor and were hesitant to enter the octopus's nest cavity—even when the octopus was not there. Previous run-ins with pygmy octopuses had taught the stomatopods to be cautious. This behavior involves retrieving the memory of the last run-in with a pgymy octopus and modifying behavior to suit the new situation.

Among their own kind, stomatopods battle for possession of burrows, which are the mantis shrimps' homes and main protection from predators. However, burrows in coral or rubble are a limited resource—there aren't enough to go around. Males may evict or even kill females competing for the same burrow. For this reason, the crustacean needs to learn to size up a burrow's occupants to tell if the burrow is worth the battle.

Roy Caldwell's research has demonstrated that mantis shrimps are capable of judging the size of a rival just by sensing the volume of chemicals in the burrow. In another study, he showed that stomatopods are also capable of deception. They can use their reputation as good fighters to strike a threatening pose called a meral spread, which drives a potential intruder away from a burrow. Even a vulnerable mantis shrimp—who has just molted (or shed the exoskeleton) and would lose a fight until his new skeleton hardens—will attempt the bluff. The key to the bluff is that newly

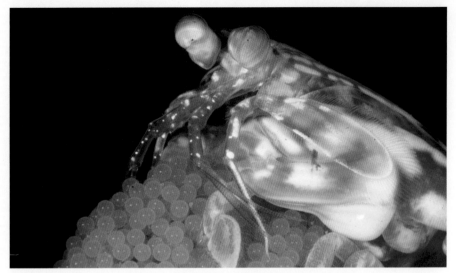

A female mantis shrimp with her eggs. She will stay with them for about three weeks to protect them and aerate them. Her mate will leave their shared burrow after the female lays the eggs, and he will remember her if he comes across her later. Memory is another sign of stomatopod intelligence.

molted animals don't look that different from animals that haven't molted, so the intruder may not be able to discern the defender's weakness.

Memory is yet another indicator of intelligence, and research suggests that stomatopods remember their mates. After they mate, Caribbean rock mantis shrimps form temporary pairs. They share a burrow temporarily. The male guards the entrance until the female lays her eggs. He will then leave and look for a new home. Meanwhile, the female stays in her burrow caring for the eggs. She stays with them for about three weeks, to protect them from predators, to make sure to remove dead eggs and parasites, and to aerate the eggs. (Developing eggs need plenty of oxygen, so the female uses her gills to fan water—which contains oxygen—over the eggs.) The male is able to remember his mate and will not evict her if he later comes upon her burrow in his search for a new home. Were he to evict the female, the eggs would die without the female's protection.

These "crustacean primates" are by far the smartest crustaceans in the ocean. Among many signs of intelligence, they are capable of deceiving other mantis shrimps, learning the chemical signatures of predators, and using memory to stay out of trouble.

MEET THE CARIBBEAN ROCK MANTIS SHRIMP

COMMON NAME: It is called the Caribbean rock mantis shrimp.

NICKNAME: Its nickname is split-thumb, for its habit of striking fishermen.

WHAT SCIENTISTS CALL IT: *Neogonodactylus bredini* (*N. bredini*), *N. oerstedii*, and *N. wennerae*

RELATIVES: More than five hundred species of mantis shrimps are known to live around the world.

HOW BIG IS IT? It is up to 2.5 inches (6 cm) long.

WHERE'S HOME? It lives in coral reefs and mangrove swamps in the Caribbean Sea.

FAVORITE FOODS: It eats smaller crustaceans and snails.

KNOWN FOR: It lives in just about any cavity, especially in dead coral.

BRAIN SIZE: The brain of a related species measures 1 mm by 1.5 mm (0.04 by 0.06 inches).

Stomatopods use a range of intelligence features, including deception, in their fighting techniques. The Caribbean rock mantis shrimp at right has lost a fight over possession of a burrow and has been evicted.

Box Jellyfish and Slime Molds

Like some other marine invertebrates, the box jellyfish has a complex visual system that functions as a form of intelligence. In fact, box jellyfish vision—with twenty-four eyes, divided equally among four clublike stalks—is more sophisticated than that of other species of jellyfish.

MEET THE BOX JELLYFISH

COMMON NAME: It is called a box jellyfish.

NICKNAMES: None

WHAT SCIENTISTS CALL THEM: *Tripedalia cystophora (T. cystophora)* and *Chiropsella bronzie (C. bronzie)*

RELATIVES: At least thirty-six species of box jellyfish live in various parts of the world.

HOW BIG IS IT? *T. cystophora* is tiny, with a bell less than half an inch (about 1 cm) in width and with tentacles almost 2 inches (4 to 5 cm) long. *C. bronzie* is bigger—1 to 2 inches across (3 to 5 cm). *C. bronzie* can have tentacles up to 3 feet (1 m) long!

WHERE'S HOME? *T. cystophora* lives among mangrove roots in the coastal waters of the Caribbean Sea. *C. bronzie* favors the coastal waters along sandy beaches of Australia. Other box jellyfish species are found in oceans the world over.

FAVORITE FOODS: *T. cystophora* hunts copepods, a relative of shrimp. *C. bronzie* feeds mostly on shrimp.

KNOWN FOR: Box jellyfish are fast swimmers that can reach speeds of 1 knot (about 1 mile, or 1.6 km, per hour). *T. cystrophora* and *C. bronzie* are harmless to humans, although some box jellyfish pack a painful sting that can be fatal.

BRAIN SIZE: It has not yet been measured.

When you think of a jellyfish, do you imagine a gelatinous blob, drifting this way and that on the ocean currents? A lot of jellyfish fit that description. But there are some that don't. The box jellyfish, or Cubomedusae, is one.

Box jellyfish live in shallow coastal waters and behave more like fish. They are active swimmers, some of them reaching speeds of one knot (1 mile, or 1.6 km, per hour) and making tight, 180-degree turns. One species, *Tripedalia cystophora (T. cystophora)*, lives among the prop, or brace, roots that support submerged mangrove trees along the coast of Puerto Rico and elsewhere in the tropics. This jellyfish is tiny, not much bigger than the eraser on the end of a pencil. Instead of a brain, it has a simple ring of nerve tissue. But most of its nerve tissue is found in its amazing eyes—all twenty-four of them!

Cubomedusae are named for their box-shaped bells, which are the jellyfish's main body structure. About halfway up the bell are four clublike structures that contain the animal's eyes. Each club has six eyes: a pair of simple pit eyes; a pair of slit eyes; and two eyes (an upper lens and a lower lens) complete with a cornea, a lens, and a retina, just like human eyes.

T. cystophora swims at the surface of coastal mangrove swamp waters. While swimming, one set of eyes looks above the water's surface to watch for predators or prey. Another set looks down into the water, maneuvering around the prop roots as it hunts a tiny shrimplike creature called a copepod. *T. cystophora* is attracted to the shafts of sunlit water where the copepods swarm in large numbers.

AN OBSTACLE COURSE FOR BOX JELLYFISH

Between 2004 and 2008, neuroscientist Anders Garm was conducting research into box jellyfish vision at Lund University in Sweden. He devised an obstacle course for box jellyfish to see how well they could avoid

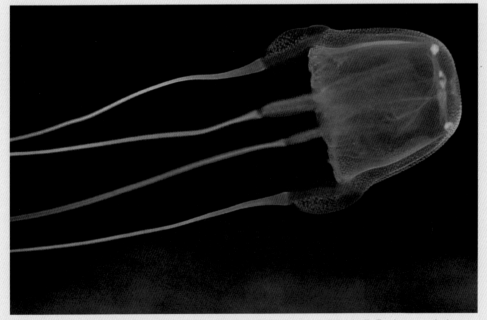

Box jellyfish have as many as fifteen tentacles at each corner of the bell. Each tentacle has thousands of stinging cells.

obstructions in their path. In a 4- by 20-inch (10 by 51 cm) flow tank (a tank with running water), he arranged clear and colored plastic cylinders. The cylinders were thin, some only 0.4 inches (1 cm) wide and some 0.8 inches (2 cm) wide. Then he tested *T. cystophora* and a different box jellyfish species from Australia known as *Chiropsella bronzie* (*C. bronzie*). The Australian box jellyfish's native habitat is the ocean along sandy beaches. Like all box jellyfish, *C. bronzie* also has eyes with a lens, a cornea, and a retina.

Both species bumped into the clear cylinders. But *T. cystophora* was much better at avoiding the colored cylinders. Even though previous experiments had shown that it was color-blind, *T. cystophora* was able to rely on the contrast between the colored cylinders and the water in the flow tank to perceive the colored cylinders.

Garm and his colleagues concluded that in evolutionary terms, *T. cystophora* had adapted to a habitat where there were a lot of things to bump into and a high cost—injury or death—for bumping into them. On the other hand, *C. bronzie*'s ocean habitat near sandy beaches meant it encountered deadly obstacles far less often, so good vision is less important for that species. *T. cystophora* was, therefore, the champion at running the obstacle course, using its vision as a form of intelligence.

KEEP AN EYE ON THE TREES

In another experiment, Garm and his colleagues investigated what *T. cystophora* does with its upper lens eyes. At their study site in Puerto Rico, they noticed that if they moved a box jellyfish 16 feet (5 m) from the shore, it quickly swam back. The experimenters devised a clear, cylinder-shaped tank with a flat bottom. They released a few *T. cystophora* into the tank. The tank was open to the sky on top so the jellyfish could see the leafy mangrove canopy with their upper lens eyes. A video camera attached to the bottom of the tank recorded all the jellyfishes' movements.

So long as they were under the mangrove canopy, all was well in jellyfish world. They continued to eat copepods. But when the scientists began to tow the tank away from the shore, the jellyfish stopped feeding and started to swim back toward the mangrove trees, running into the clear wall of the tank. The scientists also discovered that when they blocked the jellyfish's view of the mangrove canopy with a white sheet, they were no longer able to navigate. They just swam randomly in any direction. Garm and his colleagues concluded that the only possible explanation was that jellyfish were using their upper lens eyes to navigate by keeping an eye on the mangrove canopy. This enables the jellyfish to hug the shoreline where their food swarms in greater numbers.

Garm argues that box jellyfish have a brain after all. It just doesn't resemble what we think of as a brain. It is distributed among the clublike structures that house the jellyfish's eyes. We aren't used to thinking of brains distributed around an animal's body like this. We, instead, expect them to be in an animal's head.

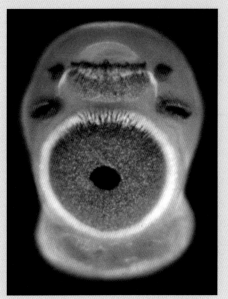

A box jellyfish eye stalk *(above)* has four eyes and a pair of complex lenses. Scientists think the jellyfish's complex visual system creates a sort of blurred vision, which aids in navigation. With blurry vision, the jellyfish focuses only on larger objects to avoid while being visually unaware of the smaller, less important objects in its path.

SLIME MOLDS

In the early 2000s, on the other side of the world, Japanese scientist Toshiyuki Nakagaki was investigating another brainless creature that is challenging how scientists view intelligence. This one wasn't an invertebrate and didn't even have a nervous system. *Physarum polycephalum*, a type of slime mold, is a simple organism called a protist, made up of only one giant cell and hundreds of nuclei. If the slime mold is big enough, it can contain thousands, even millions of nuclei. Slime molds are colorful shape-shifters. They lack chlorophyll (a green pigment), so they come in every color except green. *Physarum* is a bright taxicab yellow. Nakagaki wanted to know whether *Physarum* could find a source of food (blocks of the nutrient known as agar) placed randomly in a maze.

MEET THE SLIME MOLD

COMMON NAME: It is called the many-headed slime mold.

NICKNAMES: Its nicknames are wolf's milk, bubblegum, and pretzel, depending on the species.

WHAT SCIENTISTS CALL IT: *Physarum polycephalum*

RELATIVES: Nine hundred species of slime molds have been identified around the world.

HOW BIG IS IT? It depends. A slime mold can be just a single cell. But when food is scarce, it joins with other slime mold cells to form one giant cell with hundreds of nuclei. Some even have millions of nuclei.

WHERE'S HOME? Scientists are still discovering all the places slime molds live. They know that they can be found in tropical forests as well as deserts.

FAVORITE FOODS: It eats bacteria and other microorganisms and nutrients in dead plant matter.

KNOWN FOR: It is known for being a colorful shape-shifter.

BRAIN SIZE: A slime mold does not have a brain.

Physarum polycephal
(slime mold)

In Nakagaki's experiment, the slime mold first explored the entire maze, mapping it by sending out tubes of yellow slime everywhere it went in search of food. The yellow tubes moved across the maze, and everywhere they moved, they left a trail of sticky slime behind. The slime appears to work as a kind of external memory, telling the slime mold where it's already been, and memory—even external memory—is one sign of intelligence.

SLIME MOLD ENGINEERS?

Physarum seem to be brilliant at finding the shortest, most efficient route between Point A and Point B. In separate experiments at Hokkaido University in Japan, at the University of the West of England in the United Kingdom, and at the Center for Naval Analyses in Virginia researchers placed oat flake food lures on flat maps of nations such as the United States *(below)* and Japan, but only in areas where major cities lie. Then *Physarum* went to work. After a few days, to get to the food flakes, *Physarum* was able to create the most efficient routes between and among the oat flake cities. Engineers may someday ask slime molds, or computer programs based on slime-mold decision making, to design highly efficient highway networks in densely populated nations.

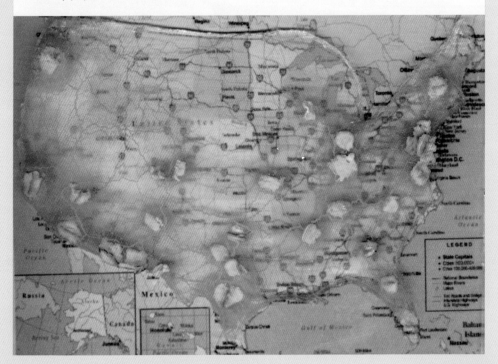

After it had mapped the maze, the *Physarum* only grew along the shortest, most efficient route to the food. It seemed to rely on the slime to remind it of the maze's dead ends. This experiment proved that *Physarum* had a primitive intelligence.

In another experiment, one of Nakagaki's students, Tetsu Saigusa, let *Physarum* crawl along a groove cut in agar. The conditions were warm, moist, and dark—conditions under which *Physarum* thrives. But at regular intervals, the researchers suddenly changed the conditions to cool and dry. *Physarum* began to anticipate the cool, dry events by crawling more slowly to conserve energy. Even when the conditions stayed warm and moist, the *Physarum* seemed to think a cool, dry period was coming and slowed down. It had memorized the experimenters' timing pattern.

Researchers such as Toshiyuki Nakagaki are pushing the boundaries of intelligence research. In his studies of slime molds, a type of single-cell organism without a brain, Nakagaki demonstrated that the slime mold can maneuver mazes, recognize other slime molds, and determine the fastest route from one point to another.

CHAPTER EIGHT

TeEny, Tiny Minds?

Tau emerald dragonflies, like other dragonflies, demonstrate intelligence through selective attention, or the ability to focus on one thing among multiple distractions. This is especially important while on the hunt for flying insects. The dragonfly brain, which is small, calculates with extreme precision so that the dragonfly can pinpoint and focus on tracking and catching a single insect.

MEET THE TAU EMERALD DRAGONFLY

COMMON NAME: It is called the tau emerald.

NICKNAME: Its nickname is the green-eyed skimmer.

WHAT SCIENTISTS CALL IT: *Hemicordulia tau* (*H. tau*)

RELATIVES: Scientists have identified almost six thousand species of dragonflies and related damselflies.

HOW BIG IS IT? The tau emerald is a little more than 2 inches (5 cm) long.

WHERE'S HOME? Southeastern Australia

FAVORITE FOODS: It eats bees, flies, and mosquitoes.

KNOWN FOR: It is known for hovering and flying backward and forward at speeds approaching 35 miles (56 kph) per hour.

BRAIN SIZE: Its brain has about one million neurons.

Invertebrates do a lot with their teeny, tiny brains. Does this mean they have teeny, tiny minds? (A mind is a set of faculties that together create a thinking, reasoning creature. The mind is distinct from the brain, which is a physical organ.)

Consider the dragonfly. Physiologists Steven Wiederman and David O'Carroll of the University of Adelaide in Australia have discovered the neuron that these aerial predators use to carry out a remarkable mental feat. They are able to pay visual attention to just one gnat amid a swarm, something scientists call selective attention.

In the wild, dragonflies have to pick out prey from a cloud of flying insects. Some of these insects (flies, mosquitoes, and gnats) are perfect food sources, while some are other dragonflies. To be successful in the hunt, a dragonfly has to be able to avoid distraction and pay attention to only a single insect, say a gnat, while ignoring other potential prey and other dragonflies. Catching the gnat is no easy task. The gnat is in constant motion. The dragonfly has to figure out how fast the gnat is flying and in what direction, and then plot a course to intercept it. If the gnat makes evasive maneuvers, the dragonfly has to be able to adjust its course mid-flight to keep up.

How does it do this? And what do dragonfly skills tell scientists about invertebrate minds and intelligence?

When Dragonflies Pay Attention

To discover the answers, Wiederman and O'Carroll inserted a glass probe only sixty nanometers wide (fifteen hundred times thinner than a human hair) into the brain of an immobilized dragonfly called a tau emerald. They wanted to target and record the activity of a single neuron in the dragonfly's midbrain. Scientists call this neuron the centrifugal small-target motion detector neuron, or CSTMD1 for short. To record the activity of the dragonfly's neuron, the scientists had to make sure the insect was completely still. So the experimenters used wax to fasten the dragonfly to a stand.

After inserting a glass probe into the neuron, Wiederman and O'Carroll played a video for the dragonfly. In the video, two tiny black boxes moved around on an LCD screen, and the glass probe recorded what the CSTMD1 neuron was doing. Wiederman and O'Carroll found that the dragonflies they tested sometimes followed one box with their eyes, sometimes the other. Sometimes the dragonflies would switch their attention from one box to the other. But they always focused on one box at a time. This feat of selective attention has previously only been recorded in primates. As a result of their dragonfly research, Wiederman and O'Carroll think the neural wiring necessary for selective attention exists in many other animal orders as well.

How Selective Attention Works

After a dragonfly singles out a potential victim using selective attention, it must choose a flight course that will intercept its prey. Dragonflies are very good at this. They intercept their intended target 95 percent of the time, and they are fast and precise. Scientists don't know the exact details of how dragonflies are able to estimate the route so quickly and so precisely, but they believe that dragonflies solve this very complex problem by employing a neat trick that indicates invertebrate brainpower.

During the approach, the dragonfly ensures that the prey stays in the center of its vision. But the attack is so short and fast that this strategy

Target-selective descending neurons (TSDNs) control a dragonfly's wings and their ability to precisely and quickly carry out an effective flight course. This is crucial in hunting flying insects, which may suddenly and rapidly change direction.

requires that dragonflies must constantly detect very small changes in the prey's direction and send this information to its own wings in under forty milliseconds. (By contrast, human muscle reaction time is 0.25 seconds.) In the early 1980s, neuroethologist Robert Olberg of Union College in New York discovered eight pairs of dragonfly neurons that appear to carry out this difficult task. (A neuroethologist is a biologist who studies the neural mechanisms behind natural behaviors.) Olberg named these neurons target-selective descending neurons, or TSDNs. In England, at Cambridge University, Paloma Gonzalez-Bellido and her neuroethologist colleagues in other countries are studying the neural code used by TSDNs to control dragonfly wings. In 2013 they showed that each TSDN is specialized to detect movement in a different direction. The TSDNs respond most strongly when the direction in which the prey is moving and the direction in which the dragonfly is moving are in sync.

To understand dragonfly skill, Gonzalez-Bellido says to do the following:

> Imagine a game in which you must use your tennis racket to
> deflect incoming balls, only you don't know where the other
> player is and the balls may come from any direction. Since you
> cannot successfully monitor all directions at the same time, you
> recruit four friends to help you. You ask that they face in different
> directions (north, south, east, and west) and that they remain silent
> whenever they do not see a ball, but to yell if they see one coming,
> and yell very loudly if they see one coming straight for them. By
> listening to all four of your friends at once, you would be able to
> figure out the direction of the incoming ball, and thus move your
> racket accordingly. Of course, the more friends looking out and
> yelling, the easier it would become for you to reliably estimate the
> direction of the ball.

In the case of dragonflies, the friends are TSDNs, which code the prey's direction and send information to the muscles that control the insect's wings. Although the brains of many species, including cockroaches and monkeys, have been shown to use a similar mathematical formula, thus far dragonflies are the champions of this computation. They are the only ones that can achieve such precision with only sixteen neurons. The dragonfly's seamless computation in midair is a sign of intelligence.

THE TARANTULA HAWK WASP MEASURES THE LOCUST

In his 2012 book about the brains of insects, spiders, and other arthropods, neuroscientist Nick Strausfeld of the University of Arizona at Tucson tells a story about being in the Arizona desert on a hot July day. He was with his wife, Camilla, who noticed a tarantula hawk wasp of the species *Pepsis thisbe*. This female spider wasp (of which five thousand species are known to exist) uses its sting to paralyze spiders and insects. The wasp then digs a hole, drags the still-living victim into the hole, lays a single egg on top, and seals the hole. The emerging wasp larva will eat the paralyzed live victim.

MEET THE TARANTULA HAWK WASP

COMMON NAME: Its name is tarantula hawk wasp.

NICKNAME: Its nickname is spider wasp.

WHAT SCIENTISTS CALL IT: *Pepsis thisbe* (*P. thisbe*)

RELATIVES: Scientists have identified almost five thousand species of spider wasps, all in the family Pompilidae.

HOW BIG IS IT? The tarantula hawk wasp averages just under 2 inches (5 cm) long.

WHERE'S HOME? American Southwest

FAVORITE FOODS: It eats tarantulas and large insects.

KNOWN FOR: It is known for creating zombies (paralyzing live prey) as food for its larvae.

BRAIN SIZE: It has not yet been measured.

Male tarantula hawk wasps *(below)* feed on the flowers of some plants and trees. The female of the species hunts spiders and insects, paralyzing them through her sting. She is quite intelligent, with an ability to analyze surroundings and to compare size to volume when hunting and dragging her prey to the hole in which she will bury it (alive) and lay her egg.

The wasp that Camilla Strausfeld noticed was digging frantically in the sandy desert soil. Eventually, the wasp flew off and returned carrying a large locust. It was so heavy that the wasp had to land and rest on the way to the hole she was digging. She set the locust down near the entrance to the hole and began to "dig in earnest. Within a few minutes . . . grains of sand were being ejected with great force. Every so often she emerged to pace forward and backward, in and out of the excavation. Then she walked over to the paralyzed [locust], straddled it, and began to walk back and forth along the length of its body before returning to the hole to dig some more," Strausfeld later wrote. The wasp repeated the pacing a few times. When the hole was deeper than the locust was long, she stopped digging and dragged her victim into the hole. Strausfeld observed, "She was measuring the length and possibly the breadth of the locust and comparing it to the volume of the hole."

The tarantula hawk wasp was demonstrating the ability to analyze her surroundings and make decisions accordingly and to compare the size of the locust with the volume of the hole. Brainpower such as this is very impressive, particularly when the animal's brain volume is slightly less than 0.0001 cubic inches (2 cu. mm).

WHY INVERTEBRATE INTELLIGENCE MATTERS

Even though some invertebrates have the ability to pay attention, few (if any) scientists think they have minds like our primate minds. One key way primate brains differ from invertebrate brains is the presence of mirror neurons, neurons that make it possible for primates, including humans, to understand the intentions of others. All the same, some scientists are asking if invertebrates have some version of a mind. Some of the leading researchers in invertebrate cognition include Martin Giurfa at the Research Centre on Animal Cognition in Toulouse, France. He collaborates with a group at Sheffield University in the United Kingdom, called the Green Brain Project, headed by James Marshall, Thomas Nowotny, Eleni Vasilaki, and Kevin Gurney. They are trying to create a robot bee to serve as a model for learning more about bee cognition.

Even though invertebrates may not have a primate-like mind, the feats of which Portia the jumping spider is capable indicate that invertebrate brains might be far more flexible and adaptable than we've given spineless creatures credit for. Invertebrates do amazing things with their mostly tiny brains: they plan elaborate detours to reach their prey, they recognize the faces of nestmates, they play with LEGO bricks, and they use tools. They cooperate as swarms and superorganisms. They maneuver around their complex environments without injuring themselves, and they focus their attention with extreme precision. They solve problems, and some of them have excellent memories. They even learn from experience and apply that knowledge to new situations.

Invertebrates benefit humans. Since 1963 the invertebrate nematode *Caenorhabditis elegans* has served in labs as a model organism for the study of the neural development of animals. *Drosophila melanogaster* (the fruit fly) has helped us learn about the basics of genetics. Honey bees and other pollinators are responsible for every third bite of food a person eats. Other invertebrates serve as the basis of the food chain.

Scientists are continuing to expand their basic research on invertebrate intelligence to learn more about the many unanswered questions about how animals think. One thing is clear: the more we learn about invertebrates and their teeny, tiny brains, the more we will see how amazing our spineless relations on the Tree of Life are—and what they have to teach us about intelligence.

Source Notes

12 Charles Darwin, *The Formation of Vegetable Mould, through the Action of Worms* (London: John Murray, 1881), 1.

12–13 Ibid., 26.

13 Ibid., 23.

19 Duane P. Harland and Robert R. Jackson, "'Eight-Legged Cats' and How They See–a Review of Recent Research on Jumping Spiders (Araneae: Salticidae)." *Cimbebasia* 16 (2000): 231.

21 Robert Jackson, e-mail communication with the author, February 17, 2014.

21 Ibid.

21 Ibid.

22 Ibid.

22–23 Ibid.

23 Ibid.

23 Ibid.

23 Duane Harland, personal communication (Skype chat) with the author, February 6, 2014.

24 Ibid.

25 University of Massachusetts, "Biologist Tracks Spider Eyes Tracking Prey," news release, October 27, 2010, http://www.umass.edu/newsoffice/article/biologist-tracks-spider-eyes-tracking-prey.

28 Ian Gleadall, e-mail communication with the author, June 21, 2014.

29 Julian Finn and Mark Norman, "Have Coconut, Will Travel," podcast transcript, April 23, 2010, http://www.latrobe.edu.au/news/videos/octopus-coconut.

31 Ibid.

31 Michael Kuba, e-mail communication with the author, April 7, 2014.

32 Sy Montgomery, "Deep Intellect," *Orion*, November/December 2001, http://www.orionmagazine.org/article/deep-intellect.

33 Jennifer Mather, e-mail communication with the author, March 24, 2014.

36 Thomas D. Seeley, *Honeybee Democracy* (Princeton, NJ: Princeton University Press, 2010), 5.

39 Ibid., 118.

46 Mark Moffett, communication with the author, June 20, 2014.

48 Stanford University, "Collective Intelligence: Ant and Brain's Neurons," news release, November 15, 1993, http://news.stanford.edu/pr/93/931115Arc3062.html.

52 Suzanne Cox, e-mail communication with the author, August 18, 2014.

53–54 Roy Caldwell, e-mail communication with the author, August 4, 2014.

56 Ibid.

56 University of Queensland, "Nature's Elegant and Efficient Vision Systems Can Detect Cancer," news release, December 5, 2014, http://www.uq.edu.au/news/node/115345.

72 Paloma Gonzalez-Bellido, e-mail communication with the author, July 30, 2014.

74 Nicholas James Strausfeld, *Arthropod Brains: Evolution, Functional Elegance, and Historical Significance* (Cambridge, MA: Harvard University Press, 2012), 307.

74 Ibid.

Glossary

aggressive mimic: an animal that adopts behaviors that deceive his prey or that lure his prey toward him

arthropod: members of this phylum have external skeletons, segmented bodies, and jointed limbs. The phylum includes insects, arachnids, myriapoda (centipedes and millipedes), and crustaceans.

baited remote underwater video (BRUV): usually a bait canister attached to a pole with a video camera nearby to allow scientists to observe marine life

biological classification: also known as scientific classification. This system was devised by Swedish botanist and naturalist Carl Linneaus (1707–1778) in his *Systema Naturae* (1735). He sorted animals and plants into kingdom, phylum, class, order, family, genus, and species. This system has been revised into modern taxonomy, the branch of biology that describes, identifies, classifies, and gives names to every organism on Earth.

brain: the center of the nervous system of both vertebrates and invertebrates, usually (but not always) located in the head

brood: the eggs, the larvae, and the pupae of a social insect colony

caste: among social insects, all members of the colony that are born into a caste, or rank, with specialized duties: worker, soldier, drone, or queen

cavitation: in liquids, a small bubble of liquid-free zone, usually created by changes in pressure. The collapsing cavitation bubble creates light, heat, and a shock wave. In a stomatopod strike, the prey is hit twice, first by the dactyl claws and then by a collapsing cavitation bubble created by the force of the strike.

cnidarian: the phylum Cnidaria including jellyfish, anemones, corals, and freshwater hydrozoans. Each of these is equipped with special stinging cells called nematocysts.

collective intelligence: a phenomenon in social insects where collaboration and competition of many individuals result in shared intelligence

colony: a group of social insects. The colony has three traits: cooperative brood care, division of labor, and overlapping generations.

control group: in experiment protocol, scientists give a treatment they want to test to one group and withhold it from another group, known as a control group. Experimenters can compare and contrast the two groups to see whether the experimental treatment has any effect.

echinoderm: the phylum Echinodermata includes starfish, sea urchins, and sea cucumbers. They all have radial symmetry, in which equal parts are arranged around a central axis.

endoskeleton: a skeletal structure on the inside of an animal's body

exoskeleton: a skeletal structure on the outside of an animal's body

ganglion: a mass of neurons usually lying outside the brain. In the case of earthworms, two fused ganglia function as its brain.

instinct: preprogrammed tendencies that are essential to a species' survival

intelligence: the ability to benefit and learn from experience and to apply that information to new situations. Key components of intelligence are memory and learning.

invertebrate: an animal in one of thirty phyla without a vertebral column, or backbone

larvae: a stage of development in animals such as insects, amphibians, mollusks, crustaceans, cnidarians, and echinoderms that undergo complete metamorphosis, with four sequential stages (egg, larva, pupa, and adult). Some insects, amphibians, and cnidarians undergo incomplete metamorphosis, emerging from the larval stage as a fully formed adult.

mind: the conscious and unconscious mental activity of an animal

mollusk: the phylum Mollusca including snails, slugs, bivalves (animal with two shells secured by a hinge), and cephalopods (the octopus, squid, nautilus, and cuttlefish). Most mollusks possess a mantle (the body of the animal containing the inner organs) and a rasping tongue called a radula.

neuron: a nerve cell, the basis of the nervous system

nomad: a person or an animal that has no fixed home and moves from place to place, often with the seasons

omnivore: an animal that eats both plants and other animals

personality: individual differences in emotions, behavior, and thinking. In animals, personality is defined according to the following traits: openness to experience, conscientiousness, extraversion, agreeableness, and neuroticism.

play: exercise or activity for amusement, which behavioral scientists suggest may function as preparation for adult life and/or for training for the unexpected

Porifera: the phylum Porifera including the sponges, most of which live in the ocean, although a few live in freshwater. The sponge's body is filled with pores and channels. The sponge forces water through its body and extracts nutrients from the water.

problem solving: in animals, to use cognition to arrive at a solution to a difficult situation

reflex: an automatic, instinctive, unlearned reaction to a stimulus

selective attention: the neurological feat of paying attention to one thing amid a crowd

social insect: an insect that lives in an interdependent way with many others of the same species. Social insects include ants, bees, wasps, termites, and thrips.

superorganism: a colony of social insects that thinks and acts as a whole, without individual input from the members of the colony

vertebrate: an animal with a vertebral column, or backbone

waggle dance: in bees, the dance performed by scouts or foragers returning to the hive to share information about a resource such as a patch of flowers or a new nest site. The dance encodes the distance to the resource as well as the direction of the resource in relation to the sun. By the degree of vigor in the dance, a bee can communicate to the other worker bees the quality of the resource.

Selected Bibliography

"About Us." AntOptima. Accessed May 27, 2014. http://www.antoptima.ch/site/en/aboutus/who.html.

"Ant Colony Optimization." AntOptima. Accessed May 27, 2014. http://www.antoptima.ch/site/en/solutions/ant.html.

Avarguès-Weber, Aurore, Adrian G. Dyer, Maud Combe, and Martin Giurfa. "Simultaneous Mastering of Two Abstract Concepts by the Miniature Brain of Bees." Edited by John G. Hildebrand. *PNAS* 109, no. 19 (2012): 7481–7486.

Cox, Suzanne M., David Schmidt, Yahya Modarres-Sadeghi, and Sheila N. Patek. "A Physical Model of the Extreme Mantis Shrimp Strike: Kinematics and Cavitation of Ninjabot." *Bioinspiration & Biomimetics* 9, no. 1 (2014.). doi:10.1088/1748-3182/9/1/016014.

Cronin, Thomas W., Roy L. Caldwell, and Justin Marshall. "Learning in Stomatopod Crustaceans." *International Journal of Comparative Psychology* 19 (2006): 297–317.

Darwin, Charles. *The Formation of Vegetable Mould through the Action of Worms.* London: John Murray, 1881. Darwin Online. Accessed November 13, 2013. http://darwin-online.org.uk/converted/pdf/1881_Worms_F1357.pdf.

Derby, Charles Dorsett. E-mail communication with the author, August 5, 2014.

Finn, Julian K, Tom Tregenza, and Mark D. Norman. "Defensive Tool Use in a Coconut-Carrying Octopus." *Current Biology* 19, no. 23 (2009): R1069–R1070.

Finn, Julian, and Mark Norman. "Have Coconut, Will Travel." Video podcast transcript, April 23, 2010. http://www.latrobe.edu.au/news/videos/octopus-coconut.

Garm, Anders, M. O'Connor, L. Parkefelt, and D. E. Nilsson. "Visually Guided Obstacle Avoidance in the Box Jellyfish *Tripedalia cystophora* and *Chiropsella bronzie.*" *Journal of Experimental Biology* 210 (2007): 3616–3623.

Garm, Anders, Magnus Oskarsson, and Dan-Eric Nilsson. "Box Jellyfish Use Terrestrial Visual Clues for Navigation." *Current Biology* 21, no. 9 (2011): 798–803.

Gonzalez-Bellido, Paloma T., Hanchuan Peng, Jinzhu Yang, Apostolos P. Georgopoulos, and Robert M. Olberg. "Eight Pairs of Descending Visual Neurons in the Dragonfly Give Wing Motor Centers Accurate Population Vector of Prey Direction." *PNAS* 110, no. 2 (2013): 696–701. Published ahead of print, December 3, 2012. doi:10.1073/pnas.1210489109.

Harland, Duane P., and Robert R. Jackson. "'Eight-Legged Cats' and How They See—a Review of Recent Research on Jumping Spiders (Araneae: Salticidae)." *Cimbebasia* 16 (2000): 231–240.

———. "Influence of Cues from the Anterior Medial Eyes of Virtual Prey on *Portia fimbriata*, an araneophagic jumping spider." *Journal of Experimental Biology* 205 (2002): 1861–1868.

Hölldobler, Bert, and E. O. Wilson. *The Superorganism: The Beauty, Elegance, and Strangeness of Insect Societies.* New York: W. W. Norton, 2009.

"Introduction to Kilobot." K-Team Mobile Robotics. Accessed August 22, 2014. http://www.k-team.com/mobile-robotics-products/kilobot/introduction.

Jabr, Ferris. "Paper Wasps Punish Phonies: A New Study Suggests Wasps Bully Peers That Misrepresent Their Fighting Abilities." *Scientific American* (blog), August 20, 2010. http://www.scientificamerican.com/article/paper-wasps-punish/.

Jackson, R. R. and A. D. Blest. "The Biology of *Portia fimbriata*, a Web-Building Jumping Spider, Utilization of Webs and Predatory Versatility." *Journal of Zoology* 196, no. 2 (1982): 255–293.

Mather, Jennifer A., Roland C. Anderson, and James B. Wood. *Octopus: The Ocean's Intelligent Invertebrate.* Portland, OR: Timber, 2010.

Mead, Kristina, and Roy Caldwell. "Mantis Shrimp: Olfactory Apparatus and Chemosensory Behavior." In *Chemical Communication in Crustaceans*, edited by Thomas Breithaupt and Martin Thiel, 219–238. New York: Springer, 2011.

"The Mechanics of Movement." Patek Lab. Accessed August 1, 2014. http://pateklab.biology.duke.edu/mechanicsofmovement.

Meinertzhagen, Ian A. "The Organisation of Invertebrate Brains: Cell, Synapses and Circuits." *Acta Zoologica* 91 (2010): 64–71.

Moffett, Mark W. *Adventures among Ants: A Global Safari with a Cast of Trillions.* Berkeley: University of California Press, 2011.

———. "Supercolonies of Billions in an Invasive Ant: What Is a Society?," *Behavorial Ecology* (2012). Accessed May 12, 2014. doi:10.1093/beheco/ars043.

Nakagaki, Toshiyuki, Hiroyasu Yamada, and Ágota Tóth. "Intelligence: Maze-Solving by an Amoeboid Organism." *Nature* 407 (2000): 470.

Norman, Mark D., Julian Finn, and Tom Treganza. "Dynamic Mimicry in an Indo-Malayan Octopus." *Proceedings of the Royal Society of London, Biology* 268, no. 1478 (2001): 1755–1758.

Saigusa, Tetsu, Atsushi Tero, Toshiyuki Nakagaki, and Yoshiki Kuramoto. "Amoebae Anticipate Periodic Events." *Physical Review Letters* 100, 018101 (2008). Accessed June 2, 2014. http://journals.aps.org/prl/abstract/10.1103/PhysRevLett.100.018101.

Seeley, Thomas D. *Honeybee Democracy.* Princeton, NJ: Princeton University Press, 2010.

Seethaler, Sherry. "Invasive Ants Territorial When Neighbors Are Not Kin." University of California–San Diego. News release, November 30, 2006. http://ucsdnews.ucsd.edu/archive/newsrel/science/santcolo.asp.

Sheehan, Michael J., and Elizabeth A. Tibbetts. "Specialized Face Learning Is Associated with Individual Recognition in Paper Wasps." *Science* 334, no. 6060 (2011): 1272–1275.

Strausfeld, Nicholas James. *Arthropod Brains: Evolution, Functional Elegance, and Historical Significance*. Cambridge, MA: Harvard University Press, 2012.

Suarez, Andrew V., David A. Holway, and Ted J. Case. "Patterns of Spread in Biological Invasions Dominated by Long-Distance Jump Dispersal: Insights from Argentine Ants." *Proceedings of the National Academy of Sciences* 98, no. 3 (2001): 1095–1100.

Thoen, Hanne H., Martin J. How, Tsyr-Huel Chiou, and Justin Marshall. "A Different Form of Color Vision in Mantis Shrimp." *Science* 343, no. 6169 (2014): 411–413.

Tibbetts, Elizabeth A., and Adrian G. Dyer. "Insects Recognize Faces Using Processing Mechanism Similar to That of Humans." *Scientific American,* December 1, 2013. http://www.scientificamerican.com/article.cfm?id=insects-recognize-faces-using-processing-mechanism-similar-to-that-of-humans.

Tibbetts, Elizabeth A., and Amanda Izzo. "Social Punishment of Dishonest Signalers Caused by Mismatch between Signal and Behavior." *Current Biology* 20, no. 18 (2010): 1637–1640.

Tsutsui, Neil D. E-mail communication with the author, May 30, 2014.

Tsutsui, Neil D., Andrew V. Suarez, David A. Holway, and Ted J. Case. "Relationships among Native and Introduced Populations of Argentine Ant (*Linepithema humile*) and the Source of Introduced Populations." *Molecular Ecology* 10 (2001): 2151–2161.

Weaver, James C., Garrett W. Milliron, Ali Miserez, Kenneth Evans-Lutterodt, Steven Herrera, Isaias Gallana, William J. Mershon, Brook Swanson, Pablo Zavattieri, Elaine DiMasi, and David Kisailus. "The Stomatopod Dactyl Club: A Formidable Damage-Tolerant Biological Hammer." *Science* 336, no. 6086 (2012): 1275–1280.

Wiederman, Steven D., and David C. O'Carroll. "Discrimination of Features in Natural Scenes by a Dragonfly Neuron." *Journal of Neuroscience* 31, no. 19 (2011): 7141–7144.

———. "Selective Attention in an Insect Visual Neuron." *Current Biology* 23, no. 2 (2013): 156–161.

Wilcox, R. S., and R. R. Jackson. "Cognitive Abilities of Araneophagic Jumping Spiders." In *Animal Cognition in Nature,* edited by Russell P. Balda, Irene Pepperberg, and Alan C. Kamill. Waltham, MA: Academic Press, 1998.

Wright, G. A., D. D. Baker, M. J. Palmer, D. Stabler, J. A. Mustard, E. F. Power, A. M. Borland, and P. C. Stevenson. "Caffeine in Floral Nectar Enhances a Pollinator's Memory of Reward." *Science* 339, no. 6124 (2013): 1202–1204.

Zappler, Georg. "Darwin's Worms." *Natural History* 67, no. 9 (1958): 488–495. Accessed November 13, 2013. http://www.naturalhistorymag.com/htmlsite/master.html?http://www.naturalhistorymag.com/htmlsite/editors_pick/1958_11_pick.html.

FOR FURTHER INFORMATION

EARTHWORMS

BBC: Earthworms
  http://www.bbc.co.uk/nature/life/Lumbricidae#p0089qqh
  These three short videos focus on earthworms in the United Kingdom. One video shows
  earthworms pulling leaves into their burrows (1:10). Another profiles Emma Sherlock,
  the worm curator at the Natural History Museum in London (4:28). A third shows how
  blackbirds stomp the ground to create vibrations (3:34).

Nardi, James. *Life in the Soil: A Guide for Naturalists and Gardeners.* Chicago: Chicago
  University Press, 2007.

Salisbury, David. "Worm Grunting on NPR." 9:23. 2011.
  http://news.vanderbilt.edu/2011/03/worm-grunting-on-npr.
  This video includes footage from the 2008 Sopchoppy, Florida, Worm Gruntin' Festival.

Stewart, Amy. *The Earth Moved: On the Remarkable Achievements of Earthworms.*
  Chapel Hill, NC: Algonquin, 2005.

JUMPING SPIDERS

Foelix, Rainer. *Biology of Spiders.* 2nd ed. New York: Oxford University Press, 2010.

How Stuff Works. "Fooled by Nature: Australian Jumping Spider." 2:46.
  http://animals.howstuffworks.com/28357-fooled-by-nature-australian-jumping-spider
  -video.htm.
  This video shows Portia deceiving two different spiders on their webs. Portia deceives
  the second spider in the same way described by Robert Jackson in chapter 2 of this book.

Levi, Herbert W. *Spiders and Their Kin.* Golden Guides series. New York: St. Martin's, 2001.

Markle, Sandra. *Jumping Spiders: Gold-Medal Stalkers.* Arachnid World series.
  Minneapolis: Lerner Publications, 2012.

OCTOPUSES

Borrell, Brendan. "Are Octopuses Smart?" *Scientific American,* February 27, 2009. http://
  www.scientificamerican.com/article/are-octopuses-smart/.

California Academy of Sciences. "Octopus Tool-Use." 1:12. Vimeo video, 2010.
  http://vimeo.com/8268896.
  This video shows the veined octopus stilt-walking and saving two coconut shells to use
  for shelter later.

Courage, Katherine Harmon. "How the Freaky Octopus Can Help Us Understand the
  Human Brain." *Wired,* October 2013. http://www.wired.com/2013/10/how-the-freaky
  -octopus-can-help-us-understand-the-human-brain/

Montogemery, Sy. "Deep Intellect." *Orion,* November/December 2011. http://www
  .orionmagazine.org/index.php/articles/article/6474/.

"The Most Intelligent Mimic Octopus in the World." 1:48. YouTube video. Posted by "FullKanal," November 4, 2010.
https://www.youtube.com/watch?v=t-LTWFnGmeg.
Featuring biologist Mark Norman, this video demonstrates how the mimic octopus mimics various venomous animals: a banded sole, a sea snake, and a lionfish.

BEES AND WASPS

Burns, Loree Griffin. *The Hive Detectives: Chronicle of a Honey Bee Catastrophe.* Scientists in the Field series. Boston: Houghton Mifflin Harcourt, 2010.

Tibbetts, Elizabeth A. and Adrian G. Dyer. "Good with Faces (Animal Behavior)." *Scientific American,* December 2013, 68–73.

"Tom Seeley: Honeybee Democracy." 57:05. Cornell University, 2012.
http://www.cornell.edu/video/tom-seeley-honeybee-democracy
Tom Seeley of Cornell University explains how honey bees go about choosing a new nest site.

"Wasps Have a Good Memory for a Face." 1:07. *New Scientist,* 2008.
http://www.newscientist.com/article/dn14776-wasps-have-a-good-memory-for-a-face
.html#.VPS-OBYZ0mQ
This video shows footage from the lab of Michael Sheehan and Elizabeth Tibbetts at the University of Michigan, detailing one of their experiments with wasps.

ANTS AND SWARM SCIENCE

Abumrad, Jad, and Robert Krulwich. "Argentine Invasion." 19:52. Radiolab podcast, July 30, 2012.
http://www.radiolab.org/story/226523-ants.
David Holway, an ecologist and evolutionary biologist from the University of California at San Diego, takes viewers to a driveway in Escondido, California, where a grisly ant battle rages. The video also features Neil Tsutsui from the University of California, Berkeley, and Mark Moffett of the National Museum of Natural History in Washington, DC.

Christensen, Jon. "Interloper Ants Keep It All in the Family." *New York Times,* August 1, 2000. http://www.nytimes.com/2000/08/01/science/interloper-ants-keep-it-all-in-the -family.html.

"The Gathering Swarms." DVD. 60:00. John Downer Productions, 2014. Included in this video are swarms of bats and bees, locusts, ants, monarch butterflies, cicadas, grunion, carp, sardines, parakeets, mayflies, penguins, and wildebeest.

Miller, Peter. "Swarm Theory." *National Geographic,* July 2007. http://ngm .nationalgeographic.com/2007/07/swarms/miller-text.

Moffett, Mark W. "War Zone: An Invasive Ant Defies the Rules of Social Evolution by Conquering California with Battles between Enormous Colonies That Act Like Separate Species." *Scientist,* May 21, 2010. http://www.the-scientist.com/?articles.view/articleNo /29040/title/War-zone/.

Yong, Ed. "How the Science of Swarms Can Help Us Fight Cancer and Predict the Future." *Wired* (blog), March 19, 2013. http://www.wired.com/2013/03/powers-of-swarms/all/.

MANTIS SHRIMPS

"Sheila Patek: The Shrimp with a Kick!" 18:23. 4th video. Ted Talks video, 2004. http://www.ted.com/talks/sheila_patek_clocks_the_fastest_animals?language=en Biologist Sheila Patek talks about her work measuring the feeding strike of the mantis shrimp, one of the fastest movements in the animal world, using video cameras recording at twenty thousand frames per second. She also explains cavitation.

Summers, Adam. "Knockout Punch: A Boxer Who Could Jab Like the Mantis Shrimp Could Win Every Match with a Single Blow." *Natural History*, July/August 2004. http://www.naturalhistorymag.com/biomechanics/082071/knockout-punch.

Tanner, K. Elizabeth. "Materials Science: Small but Extremely Tough." *Science* 336 (2012): 1237–1238.

BOX JELLIES AND SLIME MOLDS

Garm, Anders. "*Tripedalia cystophora* in the Mangroves." 0:23. Vimeo video, 2014. https://vimeo.com/112035956.
This brief video shows *T. cystophora* in its natural habitat.

Gowell, Elizabeth. *Amazing Jellies: Jewels of the Sea*. A New England Aquarium Book series. Piermont, NH: Bunker Hill, 2004.

"Heather Barnett: What Humans Can Learn From Semi-Intelligent Slime." 12:11. Ted Talks video, 2014.
http://www.ted.com/talks/heather_barnett_what_humans_can_learn_from_semi_intelligent_slime_1.
Artist Heather Barnett talks about her collaborations with scientists to explore slime mold smarts.

Jabr, Ferris. "How Brainless Slime Molds Redefine Intelligence." *Scientific American*, November 7, 2012. http://www.scientificamerican.com/article/brainless-slime-molds.

DRAGONFLIES

Angier, Natalie. "Nature's Drone, Pretty and Deadly." *New York Times*, April 1, 2013. http://www.nytimes.com/2013/04/02/science/dragonflies-natures-deadly-drone-but-prettier.html

"Dragonflies Have Human-Like 'Selective Attention,'" University of Adelaide, news release, December 21, 2012, http://www.adelaide.edu.au/news/news58341.html.

"Dragonflies Have Human-Like 'Selective Attention.'" 0:20. YouTube video, 2012. http://youtu.be/iyMU6wfSBTI
This video documents a dragonfly intercepting a gnat.

INDEX

ABOUT THE AUTHOR

Ann Downer was born in Virginia and spent part of her childhood in the Philippines and in Thailand. She worked on many books about invertebrates when she was a life science editor for Harvard University Press. She is the author of fantasy novels for young readers and of several books about science, including the award-winning YA nonfiction titles *Wild Animal Neighbors: Sharing Our Urban World* and *Elephant Talk: The Surprising Science of Elephant Communication*, both for Twenty-First Century Books. Downer lives outside Boston, Massachusetts, with her husband and teenage son.

AUTHOR ACKNOWLEDGMENTS

All institutions are in the United States unless otherwise noted.

Introduction: Aurore Avarguès-Weber, University of London, United Kingdom; Ian Meinertzhagen, Dalhousie University, Canada. *Earthworms:* Tim Berra, Ohio State University; Janet Browne and Katie Ericsen Baca, Harvard University. *Portia the jumping spider:* Robert R. Jackson, University of Canterbury, New Zealand; Duane Harland, AgResearch–Lincoln Campus, New Zealand; Elizabeth Jakob, University of Massachusetts Amherst. *Octopus:* Lauren de Vos, Save Our Seas, South Africa; Julian Finn, Museum Victoria, Australia; Ian Gleadall, Tohoku University, Japan; Michael Kuba, Max Planck Institute for Brain Research, Germany; Jennifer Mather, University of Lethbridge, Canada. *Honey bees and paper wasps:* Thomas D. Seeley, Cornell University; Elizabeth Tibbetts, University of Michigan; Sean O'Donnell, Drexel University. *Argentine ants:* Mark W. Moffett, Smithsonian (National Museum of Natural History); Mike Rubenstein, Harvard University; Neil Tsutsui, University of California, Berkeley. *Mantis shrimp:* Jay Bradley, National Aquarium, Baltimore; Roy L. Caldwell, University of California, Berkeley; Suzanne Cox, University of Massachusetts Amherst; Charles Derby, George State University; Michael F. Land, University of Sussex, U.; Sheila N. Patek, Duke University. *Box jellyfish:* Anders Garm, Lund University, Sweden. *Slime mold:* Toshiyuki Nakagaki, Hokkaido University, Japan. *Dragonflies:* Steven Wiederman, University of Adelaide, Australia; David O'Carroll, University of Adelaide, Australia; Paloma T. Conzalez-Bellido, University of Cambridge, United Kingdom.

Any errors that remain are my own.

A big shout-out to Mary Sears at the Ernst Mayr Library at Harvard for tracking down the nationality of an earthworm researcher and many other favors.

I would also like to thank my fabulous editor at Twenty-First Century Books, Domenica Di Piazza. She did yeoman's work on this manuscript and made it a better book in so many ways.

Photo Acknowledgments

The images in this book are used with the permission of: © iStockphoto.com/Prill Mediendesign & Fotografie (water background); © Sprint/CORBIS, p. 1; © Thomas J. Peterson/Alamy, p. 2; © Henrik Sorensen/Stone/Getty Images, p. 3; © Heike Falkenberg/ Dreamstime.com, p. 5; © Laura Westlund/Independent Picture Service, pp. 7, 9 (sea sponge); © iStockphoto.com/gnagel, p. 8; © iStockphoto.com/mstay, p. 9 (worm); © iStockphoto.com/ Kathy Konkle, p. 9 (crab, seashells); © martin951/Shutterstock.com, p. 9 (starfish); © EliRat/ Shutterstock.com, p. 9 (jellyfish); © Ipcreeper/Dreamstime.com, p. 10; © Print Collector/ Hulton Archive/Getty Images, p. 13; © Natural History Magazine, Inc., 1958, p. 15 (all); © Bettmann/CORBIS, p. 16; AP Photo/Phil Coale, p. 17; © Ch'ien Lee/Minden Pictures, p. 18; © Mark Moffett/Minden Pictures/Getty Images, pp. 20, 45, 73; © Minden Pictures/ SuperStock, p. 22; © Jurgen Otto, p. 24; © Juniors/SuperStock, p. 26; © Mike Veitch/Alamy, p. 29; © Jonathan Bird/Photolibrary/Getty Images, p. 30; © Michael Kuba, p. 32; © iStock/ Thinkstock, p. 34; © Mira/Alamy, p. 37; © Scott Camazine/Science Source/Getty Images, p. 38; © David Wrobel/Visuals Unlimited/CORBIS, p. 40; © Elizabeth Tibbetts, pp. 41, 43; © Thomas J. Peterson/Alamy, p. 46; © Michael Rubenstein/Harvard University, p. 49; © Roy Caldwell, pp. 50, 54, 56, 58, 59; © Journal Bioinspiration and Biomimetics/IOP Publishing, p. 52; © Kelvin Aitken/VWPICS/Visual&Written SL/Alamy, p. 60; © EPA/NIC BOTHMA/CORBIS, p. 62; © Dan-E. Nilsson, p. 64; Jerry Kirkhart/Wikimedia Commons (CC BY 2.0), p. 65; © Andrew Adamatzky, p. 66; © Shingo ITO/AFP/Getty Images, p. 67; © Flagstaffotos/Photos, p. 68; © Zoonar GmbH/Alamy, p. 71; © Scott Sanders/Shutterstock. com, p. 88.

Front cover: © Sprint/CORBIS (top left), (top right); © Henrik Sorensen/Stone/Getty Images (bottom); © iStockphoto.com/Prill Mediendesign & Fotografie (background).

Back cover: © Henrik Sorensen/Stone/Getty Images; © iStockphoto.com/Prill Mediendesign & Fotografie (background).

Jacket flaps: © Clarence Holmes Wildlife/Alamy (wasp); © Roy Caldwell (mantis shrimp).